Country Towns
of
PENNSYLVANIA

Country Towns
of
PENNSYLVANIA

Marcus Schneck

illustrated by
Cliff Winner

Country Roads Press
CASTINE, MAINE

Country Towns of Pennsylvania
© 1994 by Marcus Schneck. All rights reserved.

Published by Country Roads Press
P.O. Box 286, Lower Main Street
Castine, Maine 04421

Text and cover design by Janet Patterson
Cover illustration by Victoria Sheridan
Illustrations by Cliff Winner
Typesetting by Typeworks

ISBN 1-56626-102-3

Library of Congress Cataloging-in-Publication Data

Schneck, Marcus.
    Country towns of Pennsylvania / Marcus Schneck ;
illustrator, Cliff Winner.
        p.   cm.
    Includes index.
    ISBN 1-56626-102-3 : $9.95
    1. Pennsylvania—Guidebooks.   2. Automobile travel—
Pennsylvania—Guidebooks.   I. Title.
F147.3.S36   1994
917.4804'43—dc20   94-26344
                                                       CIP

Printed in the United States of America.
10   9   8   7   6   5   4   3   2   1

To my son, Casey

Contents

Introduction

I can't remember a time when I didn't feel a certain beckoning towards the small towns of Pennsylvania. The downtowns, particularly those with town squares and shopper-filled business districts, felt so very much alive. The block parties and Old Home Week celebrations brought an especially festive and exciting atmosphere into the community. The history of the place seemed to be so firmly ingrained in the culture and lives of the people. Neighbors knew each other and visited over the fence daily or continued crosstown acquaintances weekly at the local A&P.

Those memories are most certainly tempered and slanted with a certain amount of nostalgia. After all, I was just a kid while my own small-town hometown in western Schuylkill County was passing from its glory days but still

A farm in Amish country

retained enough activity to excite a small child. And now, as I approach the beginning of my fourth decade, I know that just like so many others in my displaced generation I'm feeling that same longing for the more connected, more neighborly, more community-oriented lifestyle that small towns of an earlier day offered.

Although I continue to search for it, I'm not certain that such a lifestyle is still waiting out there to be rediscovered, nurtured, and cherished. I hope it is. Otherwise, I'm on some sort of Don Quixote-type quest.

I think I've seen glimmers of what I'm talking about in small towns where I've lived or visited across the state over the years, and I believe I've found an essence of it in many of the towns I included in this book. All those glimmers came rushing out of the recesses of my memory when I was asked to write a book highlighting some of the Keystone State's small towns. Some I was able to use. Others, it turned out, were false memories, fanned from tiny embers into something much brighter than they had ever been in life.

Many of the towns you're about to discover have been a part of my life to one extent or another at different times and under different circumstances. Others are new to my acquaintance, suggested to me for various reasons as I planned the book. All of them have something special to offer each one of us, whether we're avid visitors of such places or more casual armchair travelers.

1

Millersburg:
Mayberry
of the North

At the south end of Millersburg, a large white-and-green sign proclaims, "Welcome to Millersburg: Small Town Perfection." It's no idle boast. Its words are not hollow. Millersburg, with its gazebo-anchored town square, is the type of town of which nostalgia and movies are made.

To visit Millersburg is to believe that somewhere in America's South there is a Mayberry protected and served by a laid-back Sheriff Andy Taylor. After all, if there's a Millersburg—and there most certainly is—there must be a Mayberry. Both are the epitome of the American small town as we like to remember that entity. No other town I've visited comes closer to that fictitious ideal than Millersburg. Whenever I walk down the wide-sidewalked, tree-lined streets of this borough on the Susquehanna

River, I half-expect to see Barney (the deputy not the dinosaur) issuing some ill-conceived traffic ticket to Aunt Bea.

Daniel Miller planned well for the namesake town he founded in the early 1800s, and the riverside community today shows the results of his efforts. Expansive public parks sheltered by towering, ancient trees line much of the shore along the Susquehanna River and the Wiconisco Creek, which empties into the river just west of the center of town. One of those wonderful, gazebo-equipped public squares forces all traffic passing through the town to maneuver around it in that fashion that gives a true homey feeling to a small town.

And the current residents of Miller's town make wonderful use of the public spaces the community offers. An event that has drawn the author back each Yuletide season for several years is the annual Christmas Sights and Sounds celebration. From late November through the end of the year, the public square and primary thorough-fares of the town are bedecked with dozens and dozens of Christmas trees and more than 20,000 lights. Christmas music and song from the Millersburg Area Community Choir fills the air. Shoppers scurry from store to store through the still-vibrant downtown business district.

The scene captures all the messages and nuances of that favorite Yuletide song "Silver Bells." Of course, Miller wasn't humming this tune when he purchased just over 979 acres in 1790 or when he began selling parcels in 1807. However, one can't help but feel that he would heartily approve of this and the other celebrations through-out the year for which his public spaces play host.

Those public spaces were not the only plans laid down by Miller. As he sold tickets to future landowners in his town—each $33 ticket entitled the buyer to one lot, which was drawn by lottery—he specified that the two primary roadways through the town would be eighty feet wide and all others would be sixty feet wide. Those were ample, even generous, amounts of space for the period.

Miller, who was born in Strasburg (covered separately in this book), built his own first dwelling in 1794 in what he planned as a new community at what today is the corner of Pine and Market Streets. It was a simple cabin, later converted to the first school in the community, where Miller taught local children. Today owned by the borough, it also once held the Johnson-Baillie Shoe Company factory.

He built another, more permanent house—a brick structure—at the southeast corner of town in 1805 and then brought his wife and children to their new home. The building has been remodeled several times since he lived there, but it still stands on the northeast corner of Pine (then Love) and Walnut Streets. In this home, until the town's first church was built in 1814, Miller—a lay Methodist minister—held weekly services. The Borough of Millersburg owns it and uses it as the community's senior citizen center, but it is registered on the Pennsylvania Inventory of Historic Places.

Miller died in October 1828 and is buried in the town's Oak Hill Cemetery. A few remnants from his life, such as his writing desk, are on display in the museum of the Historical Society of Millersburg and Upper Paxton Township. Some of the other displays vary annually. For 1994, the schools of the area and Millersburg's shoe companies, at one time the largest source of employment in the town, were featured.

The pre-Miller occupants of the region also are

3

prominently featured through a display of Native American artifacts uncovered over the years. The native peoples recognized many of the same features in this riverside area that attracted Miller. They frequented the region for centuries and left behind an extensive, if physical rather than written, record of their occupation. Over the years there has been a great deal of regional interest in unearthing and collecting their artifacts. The historical society has responded with a fact-filled brochure on "The Indians of Millersburg and Upper Paxton Township," free for the taking.

In occupying these lands of the Native Americans, Miller also situated his town well to take advantage of contemporary and future trends in transportation. The site is a natural landing for the Susquehanna River, which was a principal trade route throughout his life, within a reasonable distance of the state capital. It's also the natural opening for the broad, agricultural Lykens Valley, which extends far to the east. Thus transportation has played a critical role in the development of the town.

The Millersburg Ferry, which dates back at least to 1817, is the most famous of these developments in transportation. Today owned by the Millersburg Ferry Boat Association, an offshoot of the Chamber of Commerce, the ferry is the last one in operation on the Susquehanna River. Its two boats, the *Roaring Bull* and the *Falcon*, are the last wooden stern-paddle-wheel ferries in the country. Each ferry can carry as many as four cars and sixty passengers. The round-trip across the Susquehanna averages about twenty minutes and generally carries as many tourists as regular day-to-day business.

The exact date when the Millersburg Ferry began operations appears to have been lost to time. When Miller

4

founded the town in 1807, he reserved for himself the rights to both the ferry and the shad fishery on the river. A sheriff's sale in 1826 transferred the ferry rights to David Kramer, who is documented historically as operating a ferry between Millersburg and Crow's Landing on the west shore of the river.

Even earlier, in 1817, there appears to have been serious discussion about a ferry at the site. George Carson, on the east shore, and Michael Crow, on the west shore, were negotiating for the use of Crow's land as a ferry landing. They had an unsigned agreement dated 1817. And, in 1820, Crow was assessed taxes on a farm, a sawmill, and a ferry.

Plenty of circumstantial evidence suggests a predecessor to Kramer, but definitive information is more readily available from the time he took over. He passed on the ferry to his sons, George and Joseph. It then passed through several owners, and in 1890 Levi McConnel bought and combined it with a competing ferry he and his brother Richard had been operating. Another succession of owners eventually placed the ferry into the hands of the Hunter and Radel families, where it remained until 1968.

Robert Wallis became the sole owner in 1972 and eventually the last owner. In early 1990, after some troubled years when it sometimes appeared that the ferry might cease operations, he sold it to Community Banks, N. A., of Millersburg, which gave it to the Millersburg Ferry Boat Association.

The first boats to ply the course of the Millersburg Ferry were large rowboats, flatboats, and other small craft propelled through the water by poles. Owners selected from among this armada according to the cargo they were asked to move across the river.

The *Enterprise*, a side-wheeler that towed a flat barge loaded with cargo, began operation in 1873. The deeper draft of this larger, heavier craft brought with it the need for the Ferry Wall, a submerged dam of rocks placed downriver of the crossing to raise the water level. The *Enterprise* was joined by the *Pointy Boat*, then the *Dinky Boat* and, in 1905, the *Defiance*, the first stern-paddle-wheeler to ply these waters. The coming of the stern-wheeler allowed the barge to be attached to the side of powered craft, making for easier and quicker docking, loading, and unloading.

At its peak the ferry required the use of four stern-wheelers. The remaining *Roaring Bull* and *Falcon* were accompanied at that time by the *Blue Goose* and the *Monarch*.

As it does with all its public property, Millersburg has centered some special events around the ferry. Each May the two boats are employed in the only Civil War battle reenactment held on riverboats. Sternwheeler Day is held in September.

But the ferry was far from the only transportation advance to benefit Millersburg. In 1834 the Lykens Valley Railroad was built with Millersburg as a terminus. The canal from Clarks Ferry downriver was completed in 1848. Additional rails connected Millersburg with Harrisburg in 1857 and Sunbury in 1858.

The town had become a transportation hub for the region, and the effect on local commerce was substantial. In 1846 the town had two stores, two taverns, and one mill, with nearly two dozen other mills nearby. By 1875 Millersburg was a bustling community of five general stores, two drugstores, one hardware store, two confectioneries, two stone- and tinware stores, two harness shops, one shoe store, one wholesale tobacco company, two banks, two hotels, two restaurants, two tanneries, two sawmills, one shingle mill, one foundry, and one newspaper.

Although issues of transportation have become less of a concern for towns everywhere because of modern technologies, Millersburg continues to maintain a stronger downtown retail center than most other small towns in Pennsylvania. All the traditional retail stores, which many other communities have lost to nearby malls, are still in operation.

Among the more unusual establishments are Leppert's 10¢ to $1 Store, an old-style variety store, complete with creaking wooden floorboards. Although the store carries a modern line of household items at prices similar to those of any chain department store, it still has the feel of what used to be known as the "Five and Ten." The aisles are tight and the shelves are basketed and jammed. The memories are still there. Another store, Tomorrow's Memories, is a well-stocked gift shop, carrying the normal fare of gift shops in towns and tourist areas across the country, but also a selection of Millersburg memorabilia.

Across the street is Gallery on the Square, yet one more example of this town's commitment to and ingenuity in maintaining both its downtown vitality and its spirit for public opportunities. In a building owned by Community Banks but given over to the Millersburg Area Art Association, artists in the region display and sell their work in a series of thematic exhibits throughout the year.

Art has been an important element of the community consciousness in Millersburg for quite some time. One of the most famous recent residents of the town was the late Ned Smith, a wildlife artist whose name will be instantly recognizable to those who regularly read outdoor magazines or collect outdoor art. For the rest of you: over a forty-five-year career, Smith illustrated thousands of magazine articles in hundreds of publications, like *National Wildlife* and *Sports Afield*, and fourteen books by some of the biggest outdoor writers ever. He also produced an extensive array of original painting.

Smith, who died in 1985 at the age of 65, was known for unrivaled accuracy in his depictions of animals and their habitats. His "Gone for the Day" column, packed with his observations of the natural world in the Millersburg area, was originally published from 1966 to 1969 in *Pennsylvania Game News*, for which he also created nearly 150 cover paintings and illustrated an untold number of articles. In 1971 the Pennsylvania Game Commission published "Gone for the Day" in book form. It has remained in print and in demand ever since, an acknowledged classic of Pennsylvania nature writing.

E. Stanley "Ned" Smith was born in Millersburg in 1919. He showed an early aptitude for art and learned about nature from his father, an amateur botanist, and his bird-watching mother. But he had no formal training as a biologist or as an artist. After graduating from high school, he took jobs at a local shoe factory but kept up with his drawing and painting, usually working from live specimens. He showed an unusual ability to capture not only the form of his subjects but also their personality and character. In 1939 he made his first major illustration sale, a cover for *Pennsylvania Angler* magazine, launching an incredible career.

In early 1993 a Millersburg-led group that also included many names familiar in Pennsylvania nature writing and wildlife management began work towards a unique center to further the legacy of this nationally recognized native son. As this book was being printed, it appeared that the Ned Smith Center for Nature and Art was about to become a physical reality. It was being planned as a merger of two traditional institutions, the nature center and the art museum. The core of the collection was to be hundreds of Smith's original paintings, drawings, field sketches, and manuscripts, donated by his widow, Marie Smith, who still resides in the town.

Several sites throughout northern Dauphin County were under consideration for the center, and it seemed likely that it could be located outside the borough. Nevertheless, a strong and continuing connection with Smith's hometown was planned as a hallmark.

Although the Ned Smith Center more than likely won't be within walking distance of the downtown, Millersburg is very much a walking town. Everything is within an easy walk. Even beyond the downtown, visitors will want to stroll down the side streets. While there are a few shops tucked away here and there along these thoroughfares, it's the varied architecture that provides the real interest here. Millersburg is an old river town, and the influences on its style have been many.

There are many wonderful examples of various architectural styles, some partially covered over with modern additions and others restored to their prime. The Victorian Manor Inn is a bed and breakfast restored to its 1871 Victorian presence. Nineteenth-century furniture, such as pedestal sinks and marble-topped dressers, adorn each guest room. The house was built by Adam Mark in the Second Empire style in 1871 and remained in the Mark family until 1986, when Skip and Sue Wingard bought it and began a four-year restoration effort.

Among the several fine restaurants and fast-food joints in Millersburg, the visitor will want to stop by Katy's Kitchen and Tea Room, in an old Victorian House a block off the square. Decorated in an intimate tea-room manner, but also showcasing collections of teddy bears and toy tractors, the restaurant features various quiches, gourmet sandwiches, and cran-apple tea.

And, on the square in Millersburg stands the lunch-wagon-like, walk-in, carry-out counter of Williams French Fries. Although they offer a large menu of sandwich specialties, including the "Barnyard" hamburger, and fried ham, and dinners, and ice cream confections, it's the french fries that nearly everyone includes in their orders. Williams makes them in the old carnival, fresh-cut style. Smother them in vinegar—at least enough to soak through the paper carton well before you finish the fries—and there's no other potato product that can compare to them. You could remove all the other fine restaurants, the ferry, the public events, everything else in Millersburg, and I feel the town would still warrant mention on the merits of these French fries alone.

2

Strasburg:
Close to Paradise

There's no disputing the fact that the impressive array of railroading memorabilia and landmarks, both life-size and scale-model, to the east of Strasburg provides the draw for the crowds that stream into the community. However, the small, southern Lancaster County town has a much broader appeal to it than those worthy, but touristy, attractions.

The small town of tree-lined streets and alleyways, surrounded on all sides by rolling farmlands, boasts the nation's longest historic district. At two-and-a-half miles in length, the district still includes half of its fifty or so original eighteenth-century log houses, as well as dozens of nineteenth-century buildings.

Among them, at 21–23 East Main Street, is the 1766 home of Dr. Everard Gruber, M.D., who served as a

11

committeeman to the Continental Congress. Another, the Cross Keys Tavern at 101 East Main Street, was built in the late 1700s and allegedly permitted patrons to ride their horses right into the building and up to the bar. The Swan Tavern at 2 Miller Street may not have catered to such a livery crowd, but it has been in continuous use as a tavern from the time it was built in the early 1790s until the present. Look closely at the shutters and their hardware on the George Duffield house at 20 East Main Street, for these are the original equipment installed when the house was built in 1793. The Pequea Works Building, at 19–21 Miller Street, was built in 1907 to house a fishing tackle factory, the first one in Pennsylvania and the largest east of Chicago until it ceased operations in 1986.

Today these buildings are used mostly as private homes and antique shops, but their revelations about the history of American architecture remain on public display. And they are easy to spot. The Strasburg Heritage Society awards plaques, which generally are prominently displayed, to homes and buildings in the historic district that are documented as having been built prior to 1925 and still maintain their architectural integrity.

At the center of the historic district is a marvel of mercantilery, the Strasburg Country Store & Creamery, built circa 1788 and maintained over the years in the jam-packed style of the traditional country store. Penny candies, country wares and crafts of every notion, and home-made ice cream are just some of the treasures to be discovered amidst its many aisles. Also in downtown Strasburg the visitor will find the Iron Horse Inn, with its fine dining reminiscent of the great railroad hotels of America and Europe in past times. Specialties include veal, seafood, and beef.

At the edge of the historic district, at 209 West Main Street, stands the headquarters of another of Strasburg's strong links to the past. Here amid the folk art, furniture, stoneware, and copper kettles from the previous two centuries, the dean of Lancaster County antique dealers holds court. Even in a town packed with antique shops in a county overflowing with them, 50 years in the business have given James Frey, Jr., a special place among his fellow dealers and collectors.

Strasburg, which was named in the early eighteenth century after France's "Cathedral City" of Strasbourg, saw its origins more than a century earlier as a strategically located stop for wagons and coaches on the Conestoga Road. That first major roadway through the region today is topped by Route 741, the primary east and west approach to the town. The Conestoga Road was the critical link between the provincial capital of Philadelphia and the western frontier of a young nation, along the eastern shore of the broad Susquehanna River. And Strasburg was a critical stop along the way.

"Many years ago, when all freighting between Philadelphia and the interior towns was done by Conestoga wagons, Strasburg was one of the principal stopping stations, and the town contained sometimes as many as eight and ten hotels and about that many stores," wrote Ellis and Evans in their History of Lancaster County, which was published in 1883 by Everts & Peck in Philadelphia.

Strasburg was again a critical link in the development of the young nation in the 1800s, as the struggle for a strong public education for all children was being waged. In a house at 8 West Main Street, which was replaced in the 1850s by the current building on the site, Thomas H.

13

Burrowes was born in 1805. A plaque on the current building marks the location. Generally acknowledged as the father of the public school system in Pennsylvania, Burrowes occupied the home while he led the effort that resulted in the 1831 legislation that appropriated state money for the first time towards the establishment of public schools.

The town was a center for education both before and during Burrowes's rise to prominence. Already in 1790 the Rev. Nathaniel Sample, D. D., was operating his theological school in Strasburg. That was followed by a "classics academy," which taught Latin, Greek, mathematics, geography, and English beginning in 1803, and two academies for girls, one opened in 1812 and the other in 1838.

Strasburg's railroading lore, which today draws hordes of tourists throughout the season, dates to 1832 and the founding of the Strasburg Railroad. Frequently referred to as "America's oldest short-line railroad," the line carries very little freight and few regular passengers between Strasburg and Paradise. (This latter terminus of the line has given rise to the railroad's nickname, "The Road to Paradise.") Instead, the coal-burning, whistling locomotives haul a short string of passenger cars, filled with train enthusiasts and tourists, on a forty-five-minute roll through the picturesque farm country.

Despite modern pressures to develop this area into everything from sprawling housing sectors to clusters of outlet stores, this is still very much Amish country. The living, continuing recollection of a more humble, closer-to-the-earth lifestyle is evident in several of their non-electric farmsteads, which can be viewed from the train. Their horse-drawn buggies are regular features at the railroad's crossings on roadways in the area. (Don't miss the chance

14

Number 90 fires up

to buy fresh produce, baked goods, and other homemade items from the many roadside stands—Amish and others—found throughout the area.)

For those who want a real "taste" of the bygone railroading days, the Lee Brenner Dining Car serves lunch and dinner. This is not an everyday event, so a call ahead for the schedule (717-687-6486) is a must for those wanting to include dining on their itinerary. If the dining car isn't serving when you plan to visit, there's always the Groff's Grove picnic area about midway along the line. The train stops here for those with boxed lunches, which you can either prepare beforehand or buy ready-to-ride in the nearby Dining Car Restaurant.

The Strasburg Railroad is a short line chartered on June 9, 1832, to run between Strasburg and Paradise, connecting with the main line of the Pennsylvania Railroad at Leaman Place Junction. It is not certain when the railroad first began operating, but the earliest records found thus far include a timetable for December 1851.

As with many much larger lines, the Strasburg Railroad eventually fell victim to progress. In the early 1900s, a trolley line was constructed between Lancaster and Strasburg, diverting most of the railroad's passenger business. The coming of trucking on highways in the 1950s removed much of the remaining freight revenue.

By 1957 most of the railroad's business was lost to these newer conveyances, and the railroad suffered from heavy storm damage to the infrastructure. Petitions for abandonment of the railroad were filed with the Interstate Commerce Commission and the state's Public Utility Commission.

But even as the end of "The Road to Paradise" seemed certain, a group of local railroad fans were working to save this last vestige of a time they remembered fondly. Led by the late Henry K. Long, a Lancaster industrialist, the group worked to rally the local citizenry to buy the line at scrap value and then to restore and operate it as a hobby. A price tag of $450 per share of stock in the young organization, however, quickly dispersed all but the most ardent supporters of the effort. It was decided that for that price the stockholder would become a vice president.

On November 1, 1958, Long presented a check for $18,000 to the Homsher Estate, and the Strasburg Railroad was reborn in name. Much of the track lay in disrepair, was covered with accumulated mud and debris, or had been washed out. A crossing at Route 741 had been paved over in a highway reconstruction project. The only operable piece of equipment was a section car. A twenty-ton gasoline locomotive needed repairs before the ICC would allow its operation. An old boxcar was rusted to the track.

The locomotive was sent by flatbed truck to Reading Railroad's shops in Reading for the necessary repairs and reconditioning. By the time it was returned to Strasburg, complete with a new coat of blue paint, No. 1 had its first job awaiting it.

Another boxcar had been discovered on the interchange line near the Pennsylvania Railroad line. It was loaded with much-needed track-maintenance equipment. On Nov. 8, the reborn railroad made its first run, picking up the boxcar and hauling it back to Strasburg. Only three days later, No. 1 had its first "paying" run, hauling a boxcar filled with grain from the junction to Strasburg for the mill there. The hat was passed to pay for the gas the engine used to make the run.

A little less than two months later, on January 4, the

Strasburg Railroad reentered the passenger business that it had exited almost forty years before. Two passenger trains made the run that Sunday, and each was filled to capacity.

It soon became apparent that the future of the railroad—the source of much-needed revenues—was in the passenger trade. To attract tourists, the company began the search for a steam locomotive and for passenger coaches that would allow larger numbers to be carried on each run.

Labor Day weekend of 1960 saw the return of steam operations to the Strasburg Railroad, with the first run of the fifty-two-year-old, seventy-eight-ton No. 31. The attraction of a ride on an actual steam-powered train proved to be an immediate success, and the railroad now has a stable of five operable steam locomotives.

Today's Strasburg Railroad follows the same four-and-a-half-mile line its earliest ancestor did at least 139 years ago. It is operated daily from mid-March through the end of November. Weekend operations commence with the first two weekends of December, when the famous Santa Claus Train makes its run, and continue through early March, except for December 26–30, when daily operations accommodate holiday tourists. The railroad carried a record number of tourists in 1989, transporting 396,300.

"It's almost like attending a play, except that our play is on a stage that moves," noted Fred Barbels, president of the Strasburg Railroad Company. "We offer a complete railroading experience. The passenger can be a part of what the artifacts were designed to do."

With the rebirth of the Strasburg Railroad, the seed for a tourism industry was planted. "It's a successful tourist railroad that runs through a pleasing setting, a countryside that looks much as it did in the heyday of railroading and the other railroad attractions grew up around it," explained Robert Emerson, director of the Railroad Museum of Pennsylvania.

The existence of the Strasburg Railroad played an even more direct part in locating the collection that Emerson oversees in Lancaster County. When the state legislature was considering the authorization of a state railroading museum, many localities naturally wanted the plum attraction. Altoona, Honesdale, and Strasburg were all areas with a rich railroading tradition. However, one of the conditions that the state placed on locating the attraction was an adjacent operating steam railroad.

The museum—which now includes more than 150,000 railroading artifacts and sixty-five locomotives and cars—began as the "Pennsylvania Railroad Collection" at the 1939–40 World's Fair in New York. The railroad company restored several "old relics" (an 1880s locomotive and seven nineteenth-century wooden passenger cars) to display next to the modern trains of the day. Here the visitor can tour acres and acres of trains, some inside and some outside. Many can be clambered on, and one, Old 1187 (a 100-year-old steam engine), can be viewed from beneath via a subterranean walkway.

The vast and colorful history of the railroad in Pennsylvania is on display at the museum, from the makeshift steam wagons of the 1820s to the sleek streamliners of the twentieth century. Passenger coaches, Pullman cars, and locomotives and cabooses of all sorts are included in the collection. There's even a transplanted railway post office, kept intact from its former days of operation but moved into the museum.

Among the many special features of the museum are the world's largest collection of motive power and rolling stock of a single corporate entity; a speed-record-setting steam locomotive (127.5 miles per hour in 1905); a working replica of the world's oldest continuously successful locomotive; and the largest collection of locomotive builders' photographs.

The overall railroading "feel" of a visit to this unique town can be continued into the night with a stay at the Red Caboose Motel. In place of the usually nondescript rooms of your average motel, this establishment has installed an array of actual train cabooses, dating from the early 1900s to 1975, on separate track next to the tracks of the Strasburg Railroad and equipped them as forty guest rooms. Although some inevitably are a bit cramped, staying in one for even a single night is an experience you'll be retelling for some time to come. The restaurant at the hotel is fittingly housed in two eighty-ton former dining cars. They're equipped with the look and sounds of the railroading days, and the fare reflects the days of the iron horse.

Back at the Strasburg Railroad depot, about a mile outside Strasburg, the visitor will find everything from restaurants to a souvenir photo booth to gift shops. These gift shops, however, are not the typical touristy type. Just about everything imaginable for the train enthusiast, both life-size and scale model, can be found on their seemingly endless shelves.

And if the railroading memorabilia at the railroad station isn't enough, there's the Choo Choo Barn and Strasburg Train Shop, part of The Shops of Traintown mini-mall a short distance back toward Strasburg. Again, if there's something about railroading, particularly model railroading, you've been looking for, you'll have an excellent chance of finding it here.

Whatever your level of enthusiasm for trains, the Choo Choo Barn will draw you in for at least half an hour. Not a minute less is required to take in the 1,700-square-foot animated "O" gauge replica of Lancaster County. A baker's dozen of model trains course through the countryside, which features 130 operating and moving scenes, such as an Amish barn-raising, a three-ring circus, and the nearby Dutch Wonderland entertainment park.

George Groff, the father of the current owner, began the display when he transformed the family's traditional, basement toy-train display at Christmastide into a 500-square-foot attraction in 1961. It then included six model trains and six animated scenes. Today it's tended, and constantly changed, by second-generation model railroader Tom Groff. The display really does live up to its billing as "the ultimate model railroad."

The history of model and toy railroading is the focus of the nearby Toy Train Museum, which was dedicated in 1977 as the headquarters and museum of the national Train Collectors Association. Hundreds of original examples of toy trains from the 1800s to the present, many extremely rare and unique, line the showcase walls of the museum, while dozens of working models course through detailed displays and scenes of all sorts.

Transportation of yet another sort is the focus of the Dutchland Collectors Auto Auction in Strasburg, one of Pennsylvania's top 200 events, as selected in 1994 by the Office of Travel Marketing in the state Department of Commerce. The auction, twenty-two years old in 1994, brings together hundreds of antique autos for two days in early October.

Just a short distance outside town stands the Gast Classic Motorcars Museum, a collection of more than fifty antique, classic, sports, and high-performance cars, mostly from the forties, fifties, and sixties. Music by Elvis and the Beach Boys is piped in to set just the right mood for viewing these memory-packed beauties.

3

Centralia:
A Tragic Lesson

From two of Pennsylvania's most prosperous, flourishing, and attractive small towns, we move completely to the other side of the spectrum, to what is most assuredly the state's most down-on-its-luck community. As a matter of fact, all of whatever luck Centralia ever had seems to have run out as this book is being published. The town may soon cease to exist as anything more than a dot on the map, if it's allowed to keep even that much of its dignity.

Centralia, which had as many as 2,000 residents in 1970 and nearly 1,500 as recently as 1983, was down to less than 50 in 1994. The town is the victim of a fire that has burned in the coal seams under the town since 1962, occasionally surfacing in one form or another to claim yet one more portion of the community or surrounding Locust Mountain countryside.

The fire began as a burn in some trash dumped into an abandoned strip mine out behind Odd Fellows Cemetery. It soon spread down into the coal seams and abandoned mines, bringing to Centralia membership in a gruesome club: Today across the United States fires are burning out of control in more than 500 abandoned coal mines and coal waste heaps. Centralia's is the worst.

The tiny, shrinking coal town may seem an unlikely choice for inclusion in this book, which generally focuses on positive things about small towns. But, from the beginning of my work on this book, I was certain that Centralia absolutely had to be included. As I walked the nearly deserted streets and gazed out over some of the surface-burn areas with smoke rising from them and smelled the sulphur-tainted air, my reasons for including the town became much more concrete and clear.

First, there may not be a Centralia, Pennsylvania, very shortly after this book comes out. Such a passing should be noted as often as possible by as many people as possible.

But there will always be a lesson for all of us in Centralia, whether it exists as a physical entity or not. There is only so much that our planet will allow us to do to it. There comes a point at which our impacts on the environment will cause a reaction. This is not a criticism or condemnation of the people of Centralia, now or in the past. They really were doing nothing different from what is a completely accepted practice throughout the region. And, in the broader context, their actions really were no different from the actions of all Americans. We all contribute to various degradations of the environment in one way or another. And, when enough of those degradations come together, we reach a point at which we've pushed too far. Earth pushes back. Centralia may be a worst-case scenario, but it's a lesson we all must consider.

My hometown is just a few miles southeast of Centralia, a couple of mountains and valleys away. I've been hearing about the plight of Centralia, it seems, for nearly my whole life. What has happened to Centralia could just as easily have happened to any small town in the coal region, including the one where I grew up.

Centralia was born in the rush by mining companies to find, develop, and exploit coal deposits throughout the anthracite region of the state. Because many of these deposits were found in remote locations, it generally made sense for the companies to establish towns right next to their collieries for the workers and their families. The companies also discovered the incredible economic benefit of owning just about everything in those towns and handling nearly the all commerce themselves, giving rise to the concept of company towns.

Thus the first person to build a home on the site of Centralia was Alexander Rea, an agent of the Locust Mountain Coal & Iron Company. He settled there in 1855 and over the next few years laid out the town and supervised the building of homes for the workers. At this point in its history Centralia was known as Centerville, but that was changed to the present derivation when the town received a post office in 1862 and found that there already was a Centerville Post Office elsewhere in the state.

The town straddled the halfway point, or nearly so, of the first road through the region. The Centre Turnpike, as today's Route 61 was then known, ran between Reading

Pennsylvania coal miner

and Sunbury. It was a toll road, and gates were erected at strategic points along its entire length.

The train arrived in 1855 and the boom days for the town were under way. Within ten years the station in Centralia was seeing twenty trains each day. Passenger service continued into and out of the town until 1938, with freight service continuing to 1966.

In its prime the town included twenty-six bars or taverns, nineteen general or grocery stores, five hotels, two banks, two theaters, and two jewelry stores. Seven different denominations had congregations and churches in the community. The school buildings included both public schools through high school and a Catholic school system. Nearly the entire economy was supported directly or indirectly by the half-dozen collieries that operated around the town.

Today it's all gone. All roads leading into Centralia are officially closed, except to local traffic. Detour signs are big and numerous. Route 61 immediately south of the town, which had been one of the best spots for viewing an affected area right from the road, has been re-routed onto the safer path of a parallel secondary road lower on the mountain that has been newly macadamized to handle the traffic.

But the roadways are closed in official designation only. They remain completely passable and are used heavily by local drivers. (The best overall view of what's left of Centralia can be had from the side of the mountain to the north of the town, as you drive south from Aristes. Just after the roadway curves over the top of the mountain and begins the descent, right across the road from the "Slippery Winter Conditions" sign, there's an overlook.)

Each of the four roadways into the town takes the

driver on a strange odyssey into a disaster, first moving through typical coal-region landscape-scarred earth, huge hills of waste soils, and trees, grasses, and wildflowers working tirelessly and patiently to recapture the land. Then, up ahead, it's obvious that we're entering a town. The trees open a bit. Curbs, crumbling as they are, begin to frame the macadam of the road.

But a town never really emerges, just some scattered houses with lots of wildflower-filled spaces between them, where neighboring buildings once stood and neighbors once lived. Individual row houses stand singly here and there, lacking the adjoining homes that give the building style its name. The schematic or layout of a town is there, with streets and sidewalks but little else.

Even when all the buildings have been torn down, this ghost of a town will remain as a stark reminder of what many feel—justified or not—was a classic example of government ineptitude. In the first twenty years of the fire's known existence, the state and federal governments spent more than $7 million in sixteen failed attempts to contain or extinguish the fire.

Although many plans were advanced to fight the blaze, it remains generally acknowledged that the only method ever proven totally effective against a fire like Centralia's is digging it out, extinguishing it, removing all combustible materials, and refilling the dig area. It is also the most expensive method. On several occasions, digging operations appeared to get to the heart of the fire only to be halted just as it seemed they could actually extinguish it. Funding had run out, the anxious residents were told.

Other methods, such as flooding the fire with slurry and fire barriers, also were tried, only to fail. Even more were dreamed up, debated, and abandoned on the basis of theory alone. One plan had water in huge volumes being dumped onto the flames. That was abandoned when it was realized the underground temperature in the fire areas is so high that the fires would simply reignite after evaporating the water.

Another rejected plan would have tried to harness the fire in a "controlled burnout" and produce electricity as a byproduct. Steel shafts lined with refractory bricks would have been lowered into the burning area, and exhaust fans would have drawn out the hot gases to drive a steam-turbine power plant. The developer of the plan estimated that sites in Centralia could have generated as much as 430 billion kilowatt hours of electricity. However, the process also could have accelerated the fire, spread the burn area faster, and led to even more cave-ins and subsidence.

Compounding the problem of failed solutions was the government bureaucracy that sprang up as agency after agency became involved, from the local to the state to the federal level. Millions of dollars were poured down blind alleys with no results beyond the nicely printed and bound reports they generated. Protest signs, posters, and banners were regular features on front porches and lawns.

Centralia had become a frustrating and frightening place in which to live. At some spots monitors recorded ground temperatures of more than 1,000 degrees Fahrenheit. Glowing hot spots were visible each night across the landscape where the fire burned to the surface. Sudden cave-ins were claiming backyards and basements as the ground above subterranean burn areas gave way. In 1979 the temperature in the underground gasoline storage tanks at the local Amoco gas station was found to be 172 degrees Fahrenheit. The owner was forced to drain the tanks to avoid an explosion.

Centralia by now had become a regular feature of the national news. So widely known was the situation in the town that Superman even paid a visit to Centralia, in a 1980 comic, using his super breath to blow out the fire.

But even less dramatic solutions to the problem now seemed to be just as fictitious and out of reach. Many homes in the town were equipped with carbon monoxide monitors that sounded an earsplitting alarm whenever the gas level inside the house reached thirty-five parts per million. A good number of residents, by now suspicious of anything that the government offered them, had taken up the traditional miners' practice of keeping canaries as an early-warning system for any deadly gases that might seep into their homes.

Then, on Valentine's Day, 1981, a near-catastrophe accelerated the push on all the government agencies for some form of relief. Todd Domboski, twelve years old, went out to investigate smoke he saw rising from his grandmother's backyard, fell into a fuming hole that suddenly opened under his feet, and was saved only because a cousin had seen the accident and was able to pull him out.

Another step toward the demise of Centralia followed shortly after that. A team of consulting engineers announced they had determined that the blaze was much worse than anyone had previously suspected. They pieced together a thermal map of the area from aerial infrared photography that showed the fire was actually moving along four fronts and in more than one major coal seam beneath the town.

Hope among the citizenry for some solution that

would extinguish the blaze and save the town sank to new lows. In October 1983, the U.S. Congress allocated $42 million to move the residents from Centralia, offering $7,000 to $35,000 for their homes, which the federal government would then demolish. There would also be relocation aid ranging from $9,300 to $15,000 per house.

The offer drove deep rifts throughout the government-weary community. Those who wanted to stay saw those who wanted to leave as fast-buck opportunists deserting a sinking ship. Those who wanted to leave saw those who wanted to stay as fools. Neighbor refused to talk to neighbor. Relative avoided relative. The state felt it necessary to locate a stress center in the town to help the people through all the confusion, bitterness, and anguish.

In a nonbinding referendum in November 1983, a majority of Centralia's residents—the population then was about 1,500—voted to give up the fight and abandon their town.

As this book went to print in 1994, the state was trying to bring the power of eminent domain to bear on the handful of residents who had yet to agree to abandon the borough. If the state's orders were held up in court, the homes would be condemned and the properties would be taken because of the dangers posed by the fire. Fourteen of the remaining "stayers" converted to the relocated ranks in the face of this new pressure from the state. That left just a few more than forty residents in the town.

For most of our other towns in this book, I've discussed a restaurant or two with some specialty on the menu or something else out of the ordinary to offer. I can't do that for Centralia. There no longer are any restaurants of any sort. The only public refreshment available is a can of soda from the machine along the side of the Speed Spot, an automotive accessory store that is the last remaining business in the town. How long that will be available is anyone's guess.

In 1981, as the Concerned Citizens Against the Centralia Mine Fire were lobbying in Washington for funding for yet another plan to deal with the problem, they carried with them a special plaque for the Secretary of the Interior, James Watt. It read "Centralia Mine Fire, 1962–19??" They said that Watt, as the leading representative of the federal government, had the power to fill in the ending date. He never did, and now, as we close the gap on the next century, we might wonder if that plaque should have read "Centralia Mine Fire, 1962–????"

By some estimates, the fire here could burn for more than 1,000 years.

4

Emlenton:
Victorian Flavor

At one time Emlenton stood on one of the primary routes north and south through the western part of the state. Travelers in the region almost always had to go through the borough to get where they were going. Today, with the region's oil boom gone bust, you almost have to go out of your way to get to Emlenton. The tiny borough of 750 or so has been passed by quite a bit in more recent days.

Emlenton lies within a stone's throw of I-80, the primary east-west thoroughfare of northern Pennsylvania, which matter-of-factly ignores the proximity to the town and offers no Emlenton exit. Nevertheless, the town is easily accessible from nearby interchanges, and it is benefiting from a growing and diverse tourist industry, ranging from antique collectors to river-bound canoeists.

The Shortway Bridge, which carries I-80 over the Allegheny River just south of the town, carries a bit of notoriety of its own, standing 270 feet above the river, the highest bridge on a major highway east of the Mississippi River.

The snubbing of Emlenton by the builders of I-80 may actually have been a blessing in disguise, at least as some of those working to grow a Victorian-façaded business district in the town see it. The billboards and neon signs that generally line exits on interstates have not come to Emlenton. It can appear that civilization went right past the town. And, in today's mass exodus from the fast-paced, stress-filled life of modern urban and suburban America, this semblance of a former, quieter time can be a real asset.

The character of the town is relatively intact, something that can't be said for many a town with an interstate interchange. That fact hasn't escaped the attention of those residents who seem to be well on their way to obtaining historic-district designation for the downtown area of Hill, Main, and Water streets. The Victorian decor remains on several homes and businesses, and others are beginning to restore their properties to the architecture of that time period.

Each year the Chamber of Commerce sponsors two old-fashioned events to raise funds for various year-long projects and local needs, such as the volunteer fire company and the Fish Food Cupboard (a fund for the needy in the area). The annual Summer Festival in July carries the subtitle "Ye Olde River Days" and is packed with such old-time events as a kiddies' parade, hayrides, and a downtown carnival. (There's also a townwide garage sale, complete with a map to help those in search of bargain treasures.) The Old-Fashioned Christmas in Oil Country is staged early each December, featuring displays and open houses at the town's three bed and breakfast inns, varied entertainment, and the special feeling that only downtown/small-town Christmas shopping can bring.

Emlenton as a town was formally laid out in 1830 on land owned by Andrew McCaslin and Joseph M. Fox, whose wife's maiden name of Emlen was appropriated for the new community. McCaslin built two houses on the bank of the river and began operating a ferry. However, the first resident of Emlenton, even before it was Emlenton, was riverman John Kerr, who built his house around 1810.

The first industry to come to Emlenton was iron. Less than a decade after the founding of the town, more than twenty iron furnaces were blasting away within a radius of a few miles. The river brought raw materials into the furnaces and transported their products to the rest of the world until the mid-1870s, when the Emlenton, Shippenville, and Clarion Railroad brought the iron horse to the town. By 1877 daily trains were running out of Emlenton.

By that time the oil and gas industries were on what appeared to be a nonstop ride to everlasting prosperity. The world's first commercially successful oil well had been drilled just thirty miles to the north in 1859 by Col. Edward Drake; natural gas had been discovered in 1872 and was now being tapped. Emlenton continued in its role as a transportation center. From the wells on the surrounding countryside, the oil was carried into town in barrels loaded onto horse-drawn wagons. There the barrels were emptied into wooden tanks on flatcars and moved to refineries in Oil City.

Population boomed with the region's industries and

transportation routes, and by 1879 the residents numbered about 1,600. In addition to a thriving business community, Emlenton then was able to support an opera house, located on the second floor of the Emlenton Bank building (now First National). In the *History of Venango County*, it was reported that Emlenton's business community at the time "felt encouraged at the future prospects of the little growing city."

The town had several fine hotels, including the Crawford House and Moran House, both of which were destroyed in some of the numerous fires that swept the community. However, the most sensational fire in Emlenton was the one that claimed Boozell's Livery Stable on Main Street. It started in a wagon loaded with hay that caught a spark as it rolled past a lighted gas jet. The driver noticed the blaze as he was entering the stable and decided he would race his team through the building and out the back doors, which unfortunately had frozen shut. The stable and all its contents, including several fine carriages, were claimed by the fire.

As the region's industries passed their heydays, so did the population. Emlenton has numbered around 750 for several decades. Although it lacks the size and expanse that it did in the boom days, the oil industry is still viable in the region, and wells can still be seen in the area. The well where oil was first discovered in 1867—No. 3 on Ritchey Run near Emlenton—is still producing, and still at its original depth with no additional drilling ever needed. As the oil craze swept the residents, several drilled right on their properties in town, some successfully. The homes of many of the industry's early million-dollar success stories also can still be seen in the town, particularly along Hill Street, most with modern renovations and alterations.

You can never tell what you might find at a garage sale

Among these is the former residence of Harry J. Crawford at Hill and Seventh streets. On Crawford's death in 1953, a local newspaper claimed that "his business ventures accounted for a large part of the prosperity of his hometown of Emlenton." Working his way up through the ranks in the local oil industry, Crawford joined around 1900 with Thomas Gregory and a combined investment of $800 in an oral-agreement partnership that grew to a net worth in the millions and included the founding in 1931 of Quaker State Motor Oil. At the time of his death, Crawford was serving on the boards of several banks in the region and as president of the First National Bank of Emlenton and the Oil City National Bank.

Crawford used portions of his considerable fortune for various philanthropies in the town and in the region during the latter years of his life. He had the Elizabeth Crawford Memorial School, one of the most up-to-date school buildings in the state at the time, built along Kerr Avenue in 1928. It is still used as an elementary school. He was a major donor to and served on the board of Grove City College, where he set up a scholarship trust fund to aid students from Emlenton and nearby towns. He also set up trusts to benefit various charitable organizations in the town and in the region.

As stately as these old mansions may be, they are not the oldest buildings in the town. Just across River Avenue from the Allegheny River rests Otto's Tavern in a building erected in 1840. Formerly known as the Valley House, it housed a hotel, billiard room, barber shop, and livery stable.

Another aspect of Emlenton's past that has been restored, refurbished, and revitalized is the former

Emlenton Milling Co. Ltd. mill on Main Street, which is enjoying a second life as a complex of antique and craft shops and eateries. The mill was erected in 1875 to grind local grains into flour. It later was converted to a feed mill. During World War II the mill was temporarily appropriated for storage by Quaker State and other local companies. After the war it returned to operation as a mill, until 1974.

In reviving the interior to accommodate stores in 1989, the Old Emlenton Mill Co. kept as many of the complex mechanisms of the mill in place as possible. As a result, shoppers can get a good look at how the mill operated. A steam-operated mill, it had 60-horsepower engines and boilers running nine sets of rollers, and could turn out 150 barrels of flour per day.

With all this effort to revitalize the historical aspects of the town, it's only fitting that Emlenton has been designated as the southern gateway to the Oil Region Heritage Park being developed in Venango and Crawford counties. This town-to-town, road-trip corridor will relate the history of the early days in the development of the oil industry. Here in Emlenton, the birthplace of Quaker State Motor Oil, one can still pick up on reflections from those earlier days.

Emlenton also will be the gateway to the Allegheny River Trail, a multiple-use trail being developed by the Allegheny Valley Trails Association that begins in Franklin at the terminus of the Samuel Justus Recreational Trail and runs south with the river. The trail will extend along a portion of the river that was added to the National Wild and Scenic Rivers system in 1992 and through various relics of the early oil industry.

Former tax rolls for the town read like a Who's Who

of early oil and gas millionaires, but one of the more famous non–oil industry residents of Emlenton was Claude Ritchey, who played second base for the Pittsburgh Pirates when they won the pennant in 1901. He did, however, marry into the oil industry. His wife was the daughter of Phillip Bayer, one of the founders of Quaker State. And his daughter was Eleanor Ritchey, an heir to the Bayer oil fortune, who created quite a stir with her will, which was revealed on her death on October 14, 1968.

Apart from two stepsisters and a stepbrother, some of whom still live in Emlenton, Eleanor was an only child with no children, as well as an heir to the Bayer oil fortune. When she died, she left the fortune of about $8 million to the 150 stray dogs with which she had spent the last years of her life in Florida. The trust fund provided for professional care for the animals for the rest of their lives. When the last dog died, the fund was to become the property of the Auburn University Veterinary Medicine School and Research Institute in Georgia. After several court actions and the death of the last of the 150 pooches, the Emlenton step-relatives did receive a share of the money.

Another noteworthy resident was Isaac Shakely, a Civil War veteran who had done time as a POW in the infamous Andersonville Prison. For one reason or another, as Shakely was considering the afterlife and his preparations for entering it, he grew unhappy with the work and the prices of local cemetery stone-carvers. His response was to spend the final years of his life before he died in 1912 carving his own tombstone from a huge piece of local mined sandstone. The headstone, exactly as he finished it, still stands in the town's cemetery.

For those who choose to come to Emlenton to view

such a storied grave marker, and the many other historical sights of the town, a lunch break at The Mill Cafe should be included on the itinerary. The specialty of the house here is buffalo burgers, made fresh from bison grown and raised on a farm just outside of town. The homemade soups and fish chowders also are worth sampling.

5

Coudersport:
A Colorful Past

Considering how out of the way Coudersport really is, it's amazing the number of real estate companies that have made the town their base of operations: more than a half dozen, with others from nearby communities also having a presence. But then, if you really consider how out of the way Coudersport is—and how sought-after places with just that description have become for both residences and getaways—the proliferation of property handlers is completely understandable.

"Downstaters" have been vacationing and moving here for years to find the casual, safer lifestyles they've lost in suburban settings. The fact that the green-and-white "Potter County—God's Country" license plates are familiar in practically all corners of the state is no coincidence. A good portion of the weekly circulation of the *Potter Leader-Enterprise*, the only newspaper published in the county, is made up of mail subscriptions to people out of the area: they want to keep up with events in the county where they may be planning to vacation and with the real estate ads for potential properties in the county.

Among the more famous transplants to Coudersport, if only for a short time before his death, was Eliot Ness, the famed "Untouchable" crime-fighter who brought down Al Capone. Although he was a native of Chicago and had spent most of his life there and in Cincinnati, he decided upon this tiny northern community when he was thinking of a place for his family.

According to John Graves, writing in 1993 in the *Potter Leader-Enterprise*, "Ness told local people that he had sought Coudersport as a quiet, clean, respectable environment in which to raise his eleven-year-old son." Ness was born to a Chicago baking family on April 19, 1903, and eventually educated in accounting at the University of Chicago. But through his contact with his sister's husband, Alexander Jamie, an FBI agent, Ness gravitated soon after college from the business world to crime-fighting, as a federal Prohibition agent.

Through a series of connections and a dislike he and Ness shared for the lawlessness that persisted in Chicago, federal prosecutor George Emerson tapped Ness to head up a task force for which the young agent could handpick his own men, those whom Ness was certain were above bribery and corruption, those who were "untouchable."

The team set about disrupting the crime syndicate's business through raid after raid on brewing and distilling operations, warehouses, and trucks. At the same time, they went after the crime bosses for tax evasion. By 1933, after three years of work by Ness's compatriots, Capone's organization had been brought down.

Ness then turned his attention to the moonshiners and their illegal stills in Kentucky, Ohio, and Tennessee, as an agent of the U.S. Alcohol Tax Unit, better known as a "revenuer." Still later, during the Great Depression, he moved to Cleveland to first take the job of public safety director and then to clean up the city's police force. He also made an unsuccessful bid to become mayor in 1948 as the Republican candidate.

It was almost twenty-five years after his Untouchable days that Ness moved to Coudersport in 1956, taking up residence in a house on Third Street, behind the Commonwealth Bank building. The house remains a private home today. In partnership with several others, Ness rented the former Gates Grocery store on South Main Street, which no longer exists, and launched Guaranty Paper and Fidelity Check, a new business based on a new method to make important business papers immune to counterfeiting by watermarking them with some new chemical.

The new process may never have been all it was promoted to be, both by Ness' partners when they attracted him into the business and by the company to potential customers. However, according to Graves, "Opinions vary as to whether the commercial venture was simply ill-advised or an outright scam. Ness is excluded by all from any guilt except by association; he suffered financially more than the others and never had a chance to recoup his losses." Ness died in 1957, more than $7,000 in debt and trying to piece together his autobiography.

For the information on Ness, I am grateful to Paul

Heimel, managing editor of the *Potter Leader-Enterprise*, who is working through his thirty years of files to write the first real biography of Ness, something that will dispel all the myth and fiction that's grown up around the man.

Ness, however famous, was nevertheless only a tiny blip on the colorful, historical time line of the community, the color of which extends right back to the day the town was founded and still is reflected in aspects of the town today. For example, astute and attuned travelers will notice that the streets in old Coudersport are very straight affairs, and if they stop to consider the situation, they will discover that the streets run with the compass instead of in all different directions. The reason for this lies in the way Coudersport was founded.

Rather than being carved up piece by piece from some previous owner's lands, the entire old town of Coudersport was planned and laid out before a single parcel was sold or a single settler had arrived. In making those plans, John Keating, manager of the Ceres Land Company, placed all the town's and the county's public buildings and the public square on what is today the west side of town. He liked the commanding view that the hill there offered of the rest of town.

He then got the town started by giving out fifty-acre homesteads to the first fifty families to settle there. He also came up with the name, using it to honor Jean Samuel Couderc, a principal of an Amsterdam bank that managed the affairs of French exiles in the tiny nearby settlement of Asylum and had directed some investment into the land company. The final *c* was dropped from Couderc's name for pronunciation.

When the first county officials were establishing the first courthouse and public square in 1833, they decided against Keating's commanding view and instead placed them on a location at the center of the town. The one man who lived on the site they chose, blacksmith Michael Hinkle, was persuaded to sell his land for the grand sum of $16. The first courthouse, built of stone, stood to the north and west of its present-day descendent.

Much of the downtown business district of Coudersport today appears to have rested on its foundations since the founding of the town. However, on May 18, 1880, the entire business district burned to the ground at a then-enormous loss of $200,000. The fire started in a small out-building behind the dry goods store of P.A. Stebbins & Brother to the west of the courthouse. Fighting the flames, which were fanned by a constantly shifting wind, with nothing more than bucket brigades, the men were able to keep the fire from spreading to the courthouse and buildings in that direction, but nothing could prevent the complete destruction of every place of business in the town. The block where the Crittendon Hotel now stands was mostly gone, and all of the square west of the courthouse was in ruins. Among the lost establishments were a bank, a millinery, a drugstore, a dentist's office, two grocery stores, a harness shop, a second dry goods store, a hardware store, two law offices, a tailor shop, an insurance office, a livery stable, a blacksmith shop, a hotel, a barber shop, an engineer's office, two restaurants, a butcher shop, and others.

Several of the burned-out businesses quickly relocated to other buildings downtown, but there wasn't nearly enough vacant space for all of them. A row of small buildings was hurriedly thrown up in the yard of the county jail to serve as temporary quarters. Many of the destroyed buildings had been replaced by fall, and within two years much of the fire area was back in pre-burn order.

Despite the prosperous and civilized character suggested by so many respectable businesses, just a couple decades earlier Coudersport was very much on the frontier of Pennsylvania. And, like frontier towns in other parts of the country, it had its wild and woolly days. Writing in his *History of Potter County Pennsylvania* in 1934, Victor Beebe relates one such period:

"For some twenty years preceding the Civil War, Potter County was infested by a gang of criminals, or rather, two gangs, one of horse thieves and one of counterfeiters. Even the meager news items found in the papers of that period make frequent mention of horse thieves in Coudersport, and Potter County came to be spoken of in the adjoining countryside as a 'horse thieves' heaven.' The horse thieves and counterfeiters worked in collusion, and there is good reason to believe that a few officials of the county were also involved in these schemes of lawlessness and robbery. Such charges were freely made in the *Potter County Journal*, but it appears that though these charges were well founded, the grafters were too sharp to be caught.

". . . What I shall now say rests on evidence that is open to some question, but which has every appearance of the truth. The horse thieves of the period from 1840 to 1860 had a place of business in a hollow emptying into the Genesee Fork of Pine Creek above West Pike. This they reached by leading their horses up the bed of the creek, leaving the main road at a barnyard adjoining the stream, the place being occupied by a man who was himself one of the gang. In this woodland retreat, a skillful operative colored the horses so that they would not be recognized. Other members of the gang led them away and sold them in Jersey Shore or Williamsport."

During that same period, Coudersport also had some much more shining moments of history. Potter County was a leading northern community in the fight against slavery, and at least a couple stops on the Underground Railroad were located here. John Mann's home in Coudersport was one. The remoteness of the region was appealing to the operators of the Underground Railroad, which helped slaves to escape their masters in the South and find freedom in the North prior to the Civil War.

Timber, again today an element in the economy of this region, held a critical and central position in the late 1800s and early 1900s. Lumber mills were a natural offshoot of the lumbering operations, but several other industries came and went in Coudersport as well. There was the Dieffenbacher heading mill, which operated from 1888 to 1933; the Davidge Mfg. Company hub and veneering factory, which operated from 1895 to 1905; the Beckman roller factory, 1890s to 1922; and the A.W. Dodge clothespin factory, 1896 to 1911.

However, with mills and lumbering crews operating throughout the county, the great forests of huge hemlock trees began to disappear. By 1920 the Potter County lumber boom, which had started a bit more than a century earlier, had run its course. The population of Coudersport and the county followed much that same course. Whereas 3,217 people had lived in Coudersport and 30,621 in the county in 1900, those numbers had plummeted to 2,740 and 17,501 by 1930. Although the forests of the region today seem dense and tall indeed, they are merely second-growth replacements for the true wilderness forests that once covered this region. A tiny pocket here and there is all that remains of the native forest.

Forests provide the setting for some of the major events each year in and around Coudersport. Tapping into the region's reputation for its abundant population of black bears, which draws hunters from across the state each year, one day of the Memorial Day weekend since 1990 has been set aside for the Spring Black Bear Round-Up, a hunt that doesn't involve any guns, or real black bears for that matter. A dozen plywood-silhouette bears are hidden within 300 yards of public roads throughout Susquehanna State Forest and State Game Lands in the county. License holders ($10) fan out across the region to locate their bears (limit one to a license holder) before the 4:00 P.M. "end of the season." At a 5:00 P.M. award ceremony, the successful "hunters" draw money-holding ($25 to $500) envelopes from a bin, the hunter with the lowest-numbered bear drawing first.

The annual God's Country Marathon, which ends in the Coudersport Area Recreation Park, is one of Pennsylvania's top 200 events, as selected in 1994 by the Office of Travel Marketing in the state Department of Commerce. The 26.2-mile run, the twentieth annual edition of which was held in 1994, follows a course from Galeton up and over 2,464-foot Denton Hill—the eastern Continental Divide of the U.S.—and down into Coudersport, through some of the most beautiful woodlands in the state. The marathon is held in early June.

In town, Coudersport residents celebrate days gone in two annual events. The Victorian Picnic is held in August on the courthouse square. Everything about the event is old-fashioned, from twenty-five-cent hot dogs to a boxed-lunch social to a Victorian costume contest. The

Keep your eyes open for black bear

Victorian Christmas Festival features dozens of brightly decorated trees surrounding the courthouse square, and downtown merchants decorating their storefronts in white Christmas lights.

The past is also celebrated in a special creation on display in the Potter County Historical Society Museum in Coudersport. Built by Herbert Bartoo, a mail carrier in the county in the 1920s, the working model of an old-time carnival includes 366 hand-carved wooden figures and seventeen rides—all whittled by hand. The project took Bartoo more than ten years to complete. The rides, including a ferris wheel and carousel, move by rawhide sewing-machine belts turned on wooden pulleys that Bartoo made on his lathe.

The Potato City Motor Inn, on Route 6, is the place to eat when visiting Coudersport; good food and lots of it. On one of my recent visits, owners Joe and Kay Bohn had just introduced something new to the Saturday dinner menu, the "Magnificent Seven" buffet, the exact items for which they planned to rotate regularly. When I last partook, it included frog legs, crab legs, steamed shrimp, prime rib, their special potatoes, baked lasagna, and hot vegetables.

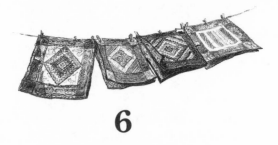

6

Woolrich:
Founded on Flannel

For generations, hunters clad in the familiar Woolrich red-and-black plaid have headed out into the woods in pursuit of white-tailed deer. In my part of the country, the first indications that the deer season was almost upon us was Woolrich outfit after Woolrich outfit, all freshly removed from protective, mothballed hanger-bags and hung on the laundry line to "air out." So common was that plaid clothing that the clothes a hunter planned to wear on the hunt came to be known as "The Woolrich," as in "time to get The Woolrich out." So durable was the fabric that fathers and even grandfathers found satisfaction in handing down their old Woolrich to the next generation of deer-slayers.

All that, of course, was before the days of "hunter orange" or "blaze orange" fabrics that many wildlife agencies, including the Pennsylvania Game Commission, now require in varying amounts on all deer hunters. Today we have the "army of orange," but not too many years ago it was the "red-and-black army."

Not too shabby a legacy for a twenty-five-year-old English immigrant arriving in Philadelphia from his native Wiltshire in 1811. John Rich spent the first three years of his life in his new country working in a woolen mill near Philadelphia before setting his sights on the wilds of north central Pennsylvania, and Clinton County specifically.

He set up his first mill in this developing region in Mill Hall, to the west of Lock Haven, and ran that mill for seven years. It seemed to be a friendly place for the textile industry, with as many as sixty weavers already operating in the region immediately around Lock Haven.

He and Daniel McCormick next established the Rich-McCormick Woolen Factory in 1830 at Plum Run (also known as Little Plum Run and Little Plum Creek) in Dunnstable Township to the east of Lock Haven, about two miles from the company's current location. (For more about that first mill, see the passage on the Olde Mill Shoppe at the end of this chapter.) They built a dam on the waterway to increase the power supplied from the small stream and operated there for fifteen years before Rich, by then the sole owner, decided to relocate to a place with a more adequate natural supply of water. He first looked to a spot about a half-mile north known as the Watering Trough. Rich planned to divert water from the Chatham Run to that new location, but ran into strong opposition from Andrew Ferguson, who was running a grist mill downstream from the proposed diversion point on the Chatham and worried that his water supply would be adversely affected by Rich's project.

Rich turned his attention further upstream to the present-day Woolrich location along the Chatham, where the greater water volume meant more power for the mill and more production. Here he purchased the 300-acre Felix Christman Tract and began construction of the new mill.

Although one or another settler may have occupied land on or near that spot prior to Rich's coming, today's Woolrich most definitely dates to the mill operator. As a matter of fact, in 1778 all settlers abandoned Clinton County in what was known as "The Big Runaway." Following a string of attacks on and killings of settlers in the region by native peoples and the British, in late 1777 and the first half of 1778, fear began to spread.

Word went out across the wilderness for all to gather at the Great Island near Lock Haven, and on July 9, 1778, an odd flotilla of anything that would float, from boats to chests to watering troughs, was packed with women and children and launched on the Susquehanna River. With the men driving the livestock along the riverbank, the party of about 200 floated downriver to the safety of Fort Augusta at Sunbury. Many returned to their homesteads after the end of the Revolutionary War in 1783.

But all that was almost a lifetime before John Rich moved his operations to the location that he first named Factoryville. That was later changed to Richville and then, well before the company began to go by the same name, to Woolrich.

Many communities throughout this region of the state, and elsewhere, grew up around such mill ownership and stewardship, but only in Woolrich did the system continue to function into the twentieth century with a company-owned store, church, school, swimming pool, park, and even a retirement home. The company's mark can be seen throughout the community, from the large community building, which could easily pass for one more of the company's complex of buildings next door, to the town's only grocery store (which recently closed its doors) in a building of that same "look."

However, for a company town, Woolrich at least seems to have been lucky enough to grow around a benevolent company. Unlike many coal-company towns elsewhere in the state, the community here does not have that raped and abandoned appearance or feel. The road leading up along Chatham Run into Woolrich is artfully lined for more than a mile by sixty-foot-tall pine trees. Woolrich Park is spacious and well appointed. The entire community has a park-like feeling to it. This is enhanced by the fact that a good portion of the town has only one means of access and egress, Park Avenue, connecting to the rest of the world to the south and ending in a gated dirt road that continues up through the Chatham Run valley to the north of town.

In Woolrich's first sixty years, Pennsylvania's lumbermen and lumbering communities—then enjoying a boom period—were the primary market for the yarns, blankets, and flannel cloth. The familiar red-and-black was patented by the company in 1864 as "lumberman's flannel." Although it became better known as clothing for the outdoorsmen after the lumber boom ended, it has remained an instantly recognizable trademark of the company ever since. However, as the twentieth century approached, woolen garments were being made in ever greater numbers, the product line was expanding, and Woolrich's market territory was spreading across the whole of the United States.

After a full century of operations, in 1930 the principals of the company finally incorporated under the name of Woolrich Woolen Mills, Inc., which was shortened to just Woolrich, Inc., in 1988.

The current woolen mill is one of the oldest in the country. It has been in continuous operation through economic ups and downs, during war and in peace, catering to an ever changing, ever expanding range of customers. And, over the years, seven generations of the Rich family have been involved in the management of the company.

The mill is completely integrated, starting with cleaned wool and moving through the dyeing, spinning, weaving, and finishing processes to arrive at fabric to be cut as needed for the company's varied product line, ranging from apparel to blankets to wall hangings. With the modern woolen mill and its nine apparel plants in Colorado, Georgia, Nebraska, and Pennsylvania, Woolrich goes through about 5 million pounds of wool each year, most of it coming from American suppliers.

Among the many outdoorspeople and adventurers who have worn Woolrich products in their exploits was Admiral Richard Byrd, the noted American explorer of polar regions. The company helped him to meet the exacting requirements of the apparel for his team to wear in its expedition to Antarctica. Jim Whittaker and his team, the first American expedition to make it to the peak of Mount Everest, also were outfitted with Woolrich apparel.

The Woolrich Store, a regular stop for many who frequent this region as a vacation or sporting spot, reflects the current wide-ranging product line. The general store area carries fine dress, recreational, and outdoor wear for all members of the family. The Classic Department harkens back to Woolrich's historic foundations with its large selection of rough wear and hunting apparel, including the traditional red-and-black plaid, Buffalo woolen shirts, and the exclusive WoolDura Cloth, all of it field-tested in the same "Big Woods" that surround and engulf the town. Seconds and irregulars, as well as selected firsts, from both of the former departments can be found at bargain prices in the Backroom. The Fabric Center offers the largest selection of fine woolens in Pennsylvania, Woolrich's own and those of other manufacturers. The Poundage Room houses remnants from the mill's cutting rooms at prices by the pound, along with a large stock of sewing accessories. And in the Cover Up Shop, there's a wide selection of woolen blankets, robes, and comforters. The store also features a five-cent-a-cup hospitality center and video presentations, narrated by Orson Welles, about wool and the Woolrich process.

The Village Cafe, a simple cafeteria-style eatery serving breakfast and lunch, is among the latest additions to the town. Adjacent to the outlet store, the café features one wall of photos depicting the Woolrich process and another of vintage and current Woolrich advertisements.

Rich's first mill on Plum Creek still stands today. It has been restored to its original condition by Kay and Don Scott, who have housed their Olde Mill Shoppe in it. Although the mill now houses an extensive selection of gift and domestic items, many of the building's original features are clearly visible. The large and numerous six-over-nine windows that lighted the various departments of the woolen mill in its first fifteen years now cast their sunlight onto the wares of the store. The entry hall and staircase to the second floor, and the store's Tasha Tudor Corner, still carry the original pattern woodwork. The floors of the second-story porches slant steeply away from the native-brick facing of the building, just as Rich had them placed to speed the runoff of water from washed fleece. And, in the building's lower-level antiques cooperative, the browser might find some item from the nineteenth century similar to those bits of daily life used by Rich himself.

Just to the south of the Olde Mill Shoppe and across the river in McElhattan, which shares the exit off Route 220 with Woolrich, is the latest addition to the region. The Bald Eagle Factory Outlets complex, with more than thirty famous-brand stores, was a major point of contention as the builders worked to get the project approved. Protest signs lined the road leading to Woolrich, as residents worried about the effect an outlet mall would have on the character of the rural region. (McElhattan, by the way, was home to one of Pennsylvania's most well-known folklorists and self-professed master hunters, Henry Shoemaker. His books on the tales of the pioneer days in the region are delightful reading.)

7

Boalsburg: Remembering the Fallen

Memorial Day was born in Boalsburg in 1864, although some other communities in other states have attempted to lay claim to it over the years.

Waterloo, New York, which has been observing Memorial Day since 1866 and maintains the Memorial Day Museum to prove it, is one of the towns that contest Boalsburg's claim. And Waterloo has the backing of the U.S. Congress, which in 1966 officially gave the honor to that community. But then, do you believe everything members of Congress tell you?

However, a version of Memorial Day was first observed in Boalsburg on July 4, 1864—two years earlier than in Waterloo—when Emma Hunter and Sophie Keller laid flowers and pine branches on the grave of Emma's father, Dr. Reuben Hunter, who had died of yellow fever contracted from his soldier patients during the Civil War. Elizabeth Myers, whose son Amos had been killed on the last day of the Battle of Gettysburg and was also buried in the cemetery, was taking advantage of the fine summer day for the same reasons and met the girls at the cemetery.

They all decided that they appreciated the mission they had come on and that they would spread some of their flowers and branches on the graves of all the war dead in the cemetery.

They further decided that they would continue the tradition each year in the future, again including the graves of all Civil War veterans buried in the cemetery. When they met the following summer, other townsfolk, who had heard of the plan, also assembled in the town square and asked the women if they could join in the observance.

Although General John Logan, commander-in-chief of the Grand Army of the Republic, established Memorial Day as May 30 in 1868, the observance was already under way in Boalsburg. Ever since that first, unnamed Memorial Day in 1864, people have gathered in the town square to make the trek to the cemetery and place flowers on the graves of dead soldiers.

The event has grown into a community event of crafts, carnival, tours of the local historic sites, live music, food stands, and picnics. Among the uniquely Boalsburg fare that visitors to the celebration will discover are asparagus soup and a refreshing raspberry shrub tea. And in recent years, the Fifth Battalion Cumberland County Militia, a reenactment group, has staged a Civil War encampment.

The Memorial Day celebration in Boalsburg is one

of Pennsylvania's top 200 events, as selected in 1994 by the Office of Travel Marketing in the state Department of Commerce. It attracts upwards of 25,000 visitors annually.

Plenty of communities claim that their events are times to relax and unwind. Boalsburg is one of these, but take it from someone who has attended at least a few Memorial Days in the tiny village, there is something relaxing about it. Even with the huge number of visitors that pack the town, I've always come away from the day feeling a bit more at ease.

But Memorial Day is just one reason to visit Boalsburg. There are many more, and principal among them is the Columbus Chapel Museum. This small stone building houses the actual chapel of the Christopher Columbus family in Spain. It was brought to Boalsburg in 1909 by Theodore Davis Boal, whose wife Mathilde de Lagarde was a niece of the Columbus family.

Although many communities across the country in 1992 staged elaborate and very expensive events to commemorate the 500th anniversary of Columbus's "discovering" of America, the only tangible links to the man in America are here in Boalsburg. On display inside the chapel are Columbus family heirlooms from the 1400s. My personal favorites among these are the admiral's desk believed to have been used by Christopher himself and an explorer's cross, which was used to claim "discovered" lands. No less impressive is the small silver reliquary that holds two pieces of what theological scholars believe was the True Cross, the cross on which Jesus Christ was crucified. When he presented the bits of wood to the Columbus family in 1817, the Bishop of Leon also presented a signed document as to their authenticity.

The collection also includes a conquistador's helmet, church relics, a Columbus family tree (complete with legitimate and illegitimate branches), and the Columbus family coat of arms. Built into the railing of the choir loft, the coat of arms includes the castle and lion of Spain's royal coat of arms, the Islands of the West Indies (for Columbus' title of Viceroy of the Indies), and anchors (for his title of Admiral of the Ocean Seas). The title was conferred on Columbus after his successful voyage across the Atlantic in 1492.

The chapel also holds several art masterpieces from the Baroque and Renaissance periods, including *The Sacrifice of Isaac* by Jose Ribera (1615) and the *Pieta* by Ambrosius Benson (1535). In the two small confessional booths in the rear of the chapel are 165,000 pages of Columbus family history, some dating back as far as 1451. Because of their historical significance, Penn State's Pattee Library has microfilmed and cataloged them all.

And, of course, the chapel itself is as inspirational as anything it holds, with all the ornate golden trim, the ancient artworks, and the setting. While the exterior is mostly Pennsylvania limestone, all of the interior and the contents are the originals from the Columbus Castle in Spain. The whole affair rests on the grounds of the Boal Mansion, home to nine generations of the Boal family, founders of the town and Penn State.

Capt. David Boal and his family emigrated from Ireland to the New World in time for him to serve with distinction in the Continental Army during the Revolutionary War. Paid with title to land in Lancaster County when he was mustered out of the army, he traded for a tract in the still-undeveloped center of the state. In 1789 he built, but never lived in, a stone cabin in what is now Boalsburg.

Where Memorial Day began

James Watson, Jacob Jack, and Michael Jack were living and working on farms in Harris Township, very close to the ground that today is Boalsburg, when Boal arrived in the area. But it was Boal who received the founder's credit and gave his name to the town.

His son, also named David, after participating in a rebellion back in their homeland of Ireland and narrowly escaping in a blanket chest on an America-bound ship, added onto that original stone cabin and also built a tavern at a nearby crossroads, around which the town of Boalsburg grew. The name Boalsburg was formally affixed in 1823, with the granting of a post office for the area.

David's great-grandson, Theodore (Terry) Davis Boal, is the clan's link to Columbus through his wife Mathilde, a Columbus family niece. He brought the Columbus Chapel to the Boal Mansion grounds. However, Terry also holds his own place in history. In 1916, as this country's struggle against Pancho Villa along the Mexican border was heating up, he organized and equipped his own military unit. They trained at a site near the Boal Mansion, called Camp Boal, which today is the site of the Pennsylvania Military Museum, and then fought against the Mexican bandit and again in World War I.

Terry's son Pierre, after retiring from the U.S. diplomatic corps in 1952, returned to Boalsburg and opened his family's mansion and the Columbus Chapel to the public. The current Boal in charge of the mansion is Christopher Lee, grandson of Pierre and the eighth generation to live on the grounds. He became director in 1966, when Pierre died.

The mansion on the grounds, also open to the public, contains furnishings that were part of the lives of these generations, the implements of day-to-day life as well as fine furniture, glassware, and clothing.

And then there's the classic American village setting of Boalsburg, with its central downtown "Diamond" town square. That setting has attracted several unique businesses, which in turn have restored their buildings to their former splendor. The result is a quaint little town with a decidedly yesteryear look and plenty of diversity to interest everyone. When Boalsburg stages one of its several annual events with craftspeople demonstrating the living arts from our past, this town takes on all the characteristics of a mini-Williamsburg.

The oldest of these buildings, built in 1811, houses Lindsay's on the Diamond. Each room is packed with a different array of specialty gift items, ranging from pottery to furniture. One is the year-round Christmas Room, featuring Old World ornaments, smokers, and nutcrackers.

Duffy's Tavern, also on the Diamond, is nearly as old—built in 1819—and even more authentic. A former stage-stop tavern, Duffy's is furnished with antiques and offers a real sense of its former life to modern diners. Specialties are steak and seafood.

Summer House, across Main Street from Duffy's, is today a Victorian-style bed and breakfast, featuring an original 1830s pine floor and floor-to-ceiling windows that open onto a wraparound porch. It was the home of Emma Hunter-Stuart, one of the founders of Memorial Day.

Today's Village Eatinghouse, a restaurant on the Diamond, is housed in a former blacksmith shop from the early 1800s. Sandwiches, salads, and soups are featured on the menu. Jacob Ferrer's original grain-cradle shop from the 1820s, just down Main Street from the Diamond, now houses a collection of antiques, collectibles, and seasonal crafts.

The other downtown shops are The Country Sampler, a collection of unique cookware, table settings, linens, and sewing needs; A Basket Full Country Store & Gift Shop, decorative accents with a country theme; The Henley House, fine women's wear; Beth Filko's Window on Main Street, dried and silk flower arrangements, and fiber, wood, and papier-mâché work by Pennsylvania artists; The Federal House, gifts, decorative accents, and learning toys; Serendipity Valley Farm, antiques, gifts, and decorative accessories; This 'N That Emporium, collectibles; The Colonel's Ladies, gifts and collectibles; Springfield House, bed and breakfast; and Ken Hull Artist Studio & Gallery and Caffe del Gatto, local watercolor artist and espresso bar.

A bit removed from most of the "public" buildings of town, but still within an easy walk of the Diamond, is the Boalsburg Heritage Museum. It's housed in the 1825 home of a local tanner and furnished throughout with pieces that were actually used in homes in Boalsburg and the immediate countryside.

Across Route 322 from the Boal grounds and the Memorial Day cemetery is the Pennsylvania Military Museum, tracing the history of the state in the military from Benjamin Franklin's first military unit through Vietnam.

The museum features a very large collection of weapons, including some that needed to be located outside the building, such as the World War II tank and field pieces. However, the highlight of a tour through the museum is a walk through the trenches of a re-created, life-size World

War I battlefield, complete with the sights and sounds of war all around.

Pennsylvania is one of a very few states to honor its soldiers with a military museum. Throughout the sixty-six-acre grounds, shrines, memorials, monuments, and plaques honor the military divisions and units that fought for the state.

8

Apollo: Moonstruck Community

$\mathbf{D}$o you remember where you were and what you were doing when Neil Armstrong first set foot on the surface of the moon? The people of Apollo sure remember, and they commemorate it the third week of June each year in the town's annual Moonlanding Celebration, which was held for the twenty-fifth time in 1994.

To refresh your memory a bit, the Apollo program was the culmination of America's efforts to fulfill President John F. Kennedy's promise on May 25, 1961, that an American would be the first to walk on the moon. It followed the Gemini program of manned spaceflight in 1966–67, during which the necessary techniques of orbiting, docking, and extravehicular activity (EVA) were developed and perfected.

All told, between July 1969 and December 1972, the Apollo program landed American astronauts on the moon six times. But it was the Apollo 11 mission that caught the fancy of a tiny town in southwestern Pennsylvania. It was that mission that first placed man on the moon.

Launched July 16, 1969, Apollo 11's lunar module *Eagle* touched the surface of the moon in the Sea of Tranquility at 4:17 P.M. EDT July 20. "Houston, Tranquility Base here. The *Eagle* has landed," reported Neil Armstrong as he and Edwin Aldrin, Jr., touched down. (Michael Collins remained in the command module *Columbia*, orbiting the moon.)

Later that day, at 10:56 P.M., Armstrong became the first man to set foot on the surface of the moon, stating, "That's one small step for [a] man, one giant leap for mankind" (NASA later reported that the word *a* had been lost in transmission).

He and Aldrin then planted the American flag and set up scientific instruments, including a seismometer that later transmitted evidence of a moonquake. They also took photographs and collected more than fifty-three pounds of rock and dirt samples. By the time they returned to the lunar module, Armstrong—first out and last back—had spent two hours thirteen minutes on the surface of the moon. The crew returned to Earth with a landing in the Pacific Ocean on July 24, 1969.

And that's the event that the residents of Apollo have commemorated since 1975 with a weeklong carnival, a parade, fireworks, and displays of moon-landing memorabilia. The event has an overall moon-landing theme, including several of the ground displays in the fireworks, such as an astronaut with a moon rock or a rocket. Zambelli International in nearby New Castle has been supplying the fireworks for the celebration since the beginning.

The town also has created a bit of moon-landing-related memorabilia of its own in the annual celebration patches it issues. The twenty-fifth anniversary patch in 1994 featured a rocket in the center with the dates 1969–94 posted above it.

But even without the celebration, Apollo is worth a look. It's one of those wonderful small towns that has retained enough historical structures to reveal the major points of its history. Promoters of the community have recognized this asset and built a historical walking tour around the special buildings.

On a spot along the Kiskimentas River known as Warren's Sleeping Ground for the trader who often camped there, the town of Warren was founded in 1816 as part of Allegheny Township. Although considerable segments of the town were lost in a fire in 1876 and the flood on St. Patrick's Day in 1936, one structure built in the year the town was founded still remains.

The Drake Log Cabin, listed on the National Register of Historic Places, has been carefully and lovingly restored by the Apollo Area Historical Society and named for Mrs. Sarah Drake, who lived in it for about fifty years. The eighteen-by-twenty-four-foot structure at the southern end of town was built between 1816 and 1848. It was purchased from Samuel Wilson, a resident of Conneaut Lake, in 1971.

Where Warren Avenue and Astronaut Way now run, the local portion of the canal system that connected Pittsburgh and Johnstown was built in 1831. This section was known as the Three-Mile Level because it was three miles from the outlet lock to the dam at Roaring Run. The forty-two-mile trip from Pittsburgh to Apollo took twelve hours. When Astronaut Way replaced the canal, engineers needed to come up with a special "floating clay" to form a solid base for the roadway.

The still-young town became a part of Kiskimentas Township in 1832, when that municipality was carved from a portion of Allegheny. Then, in 1848, the town became a borough, under the new name of Apollo. It was well into the next century, 1925 to be exact, before the borough erected its first municipal building. The commercial-style structure located at the corner of Fourth Street and North Pennsylvania Avenue is also one of the few buildings in the borough designed by professional architects. The oldest remaining brick house in the community was built around this same time, actually 1850. Originally the home of Dr. William McCullough, the five-bay I-frame house stands at the corner of First Street and South Pennsylvania Avenue.

As with so many of the small towns in southwestern Pennsylvania, steel was the most important industry in Apollo for nearly a century. Sheet steel was the primary Apollo product. From 1855 into the early 1950s, a considerable number of the residents were employed in the various steel mills in the town. Among the companies were American Sheet and Tin Plate Co., American Sheet Steel Co., Apollo Iron and Steel Co., Apollo Steel Co., Kuntz and McClintock, Laufman and McElroy, Rogers and Burchfield, and Volta Iron and Steel Co.

The booming population of the town and its steel industries led to the construction of a grand four-story hotel, then the Chambers House on First Street, in 1889. Today the three-story Chambers Hotel occupies the site. It's the same building, but without the fourth floor. That was removed in 1948 after being gutted by fire.

In the same year the Chambers House was built, the local chapter of the Women's Christian Temperance Union (WCTU) was formed. So strong was the local organization that in 1919 it built a large, brick headquarters building on Second Street. That Greek Revival–style building later served as the first public library in the town and the county. Today it houses the Apollo Area Historical Society.

The passing of the boom days for the steel industry hit the town's economy hard, as it did in most of the towns of the region. Some of the former steel plants still stand along the Kiskimentas River at the northwest side of town.

Logging and mining also were important industries in and around Apollo, and the scars of their operations can be seen on the landscape. A local organization working to correct some of that damage and allow Mother Nature to heal herself is the Roaring Run Watershed Association. The railroad grade that runs out of the south end of town from the terminus of Canal Street and then along the Kiskimentas River, for three and a half miles upriver to the mouth of Roaring Run, is owned and protected by the association. The prized trillium is one of many native plant species found here, along with a wide variety of wildlife, including many riverine species. Members of the association have built the Roaring Run Trail along a mile and a half of the sanctuary.

Yet one more of the town's historic buildings deserves mention. That's the carriage house on Terrace Avenue. Built in 1883, with the first indoor bathroom in Apollo, this was the carriage house of General Samuel Jackson. He was a commander in the Civil War, later elected to the state House of Representatives and Senate,

On an Apollo mission

and in 1893 appointed state treasurer. He also helped to organize the Apollo Trust Company. Incidentally, General Jackson was the grandfather of actor Jimmy Stewart.

Although Moonlanding Celebration is Apollo's most unusual annual event, the town and its various organizations also hold a Heritage Festival and a flea market in June, an old-fashioned Fourth of July celebration, and Breakfast with Santa in December. The former Apollo High School building along North Second Street houses 2nd Stage, a nonprofit cultural center that presents plays, concerts, dinner theater, dinner mystery plays, musicals, and other such events throughout the year. The town is also one of the stops on the annual Crooked Creek Pony Express Ride in August.

9

Mifflinburg: Buggy Town

In another age, a century or so ago, Mifflinburg was known as "Buggy Town." The horse-drawn-buggy industry began in the town by the mid-1800s, and soon the community's entire economy in one way or another was geared to the construction of buggies, which were produced in greater numbers in Mifflinburg than in any other community of similar size anywhere in the United States. Between 1890 and 1920, the town was home to as many as fifty different buggy works, and its quality products were being sold as far away as South Carolina.

The incredible production coming out of such a small town—population 1560 in 1910—was the result of good old American competition. As the industry came into its own, three of Mifflinburg's larger buggy manufacturers, Alfred

Hopp, Harry Blair, and Robert Gutelius, merged their operations and resources into the Mifflinburg Buggy Company, which instantly became the largest and best-equipped buggy works in town. But, by 1903, Hopp had decided to break away from his partners to form his own works, thus planting the seed for some pretty hot competition. In 1910, the production to come out of Mifflinburg was reported to be 5,000 buggies.

Not only the quality of Mifflinburg buggies fueled such enterprise. The sales tactics of the owners and their representatives went a long way to this end as well. Tales such as the following are not uncommon: One snowy winter day, Hopp and an employee set out for Shamokin—about thirty miles to the southeast and across the wide Susquehanna River—towing a string of brand-new buggy-sleighs behind Hopp's own horse-drawn sleigh. On the return trip, his horse pulled only old Alfred and his fellow on some barrel staves. They had sold all the sleighs, including their own.

The incredible industry that brought such quick growth to a small town saw its local start in the 1840s. Local historian R. V. B. Lincoln, a relative of the assassinated president, traced the origins to 1841 and John Stitzer. But others credit it to George Swentzel in 1847. Whichever of these men, if either of them, was the true originator of buggy making in Mifflinburg, neither remained to see the boom days for the industry. Both had moved on by then.

Nevertheless, the industry they had pioneered in the town was now moving ahead on a power all its own. The 1855 tax rolls for the town already included eight different buggy operations. It was a wonderful boom for a small town, but it was also short-lived. When horseless carriages were replacing horse-drawn buggies, in the early 1900s, many of the community's buggy works became manufacturers of wooden truck bodies. By 1920 Mifflinburg had just five operating buggy shops. Together they employed only thirty-two workers.

But as bleak as the future for Mifflinburg and its buggy builders looked at that point, when more than 9 million automobiles were already being built each year in the United States, reports of the death of either were at least a bit premature. Under the leadership of William Sterling, the Mifflinburg Buggy Company was already several years into the process of carving out a niche in the post-buggy world. As early as 1913, the company turned out the first autobus made in Mifflinburg, followed it up with several more the next year, and then began to take on custom jobs on truck bodies.

The local newspaper of the day, *The Telegraph*, was excited about the new industry for the town but continued to support the buggy industry as a whole. Pointing to the rising number of accidents that the horseless carriage was causing and noting that even in Detroit horse-drawn wagons were used to move the car parts along the assembly line, the newspaper claimed that "Buggy Town remains applicable for Mifflinburg."

In 1917 the company reorganized under the name Mifflinburg Body Company. Within another four years, most of the workers who had lost their jobs with the collapse of the buggy industry were back at work. In the mid-1920s, more than 500 employees were turning out more than 10,000 truck bodies per year.

And then, just as the local economy was getting back to a semblance of its former self, in 1929 the Great Depression dealt the final blow to Mifflinburg's major

Mifflinburg is "Buggy Town"

industry, just as it did to many other small-town industries all across the country.

The Mifflinburg Buggy Museum, housed in a buggy shop that was never dismantled after the heyday passed (the William A. Heiss Coach Works), preserves that era today. The museum, listed on the National Register of Historic Places, is the love and the work of the Mifflinburg Buggy Museum Association, which was organized in 1978 to preserve the Heiss shop and to commemorate the horse-and-buggy area. When the shop was rediscovered in 1978, its shop, showroom, and house—the three original buildings of the operation—were intact, but desperately in need of repair and renovation before the idea of visitors could be entertained.

Much of the restoration has been completed, and the museum is now open from 1:00 to 5:00 P.M. Thursday through Sunday, May through mid-September. The Museum Association is working to recreate the 1912 appearance of the buildings—a point ten years before they were last used. Many of the original furnishings of the house have been located and returned to their former positions. Several buggies that were made in Mifflinburg have been put on display in the showroom.

In the shop the entire process of buggy making can be viewed, step-by-step. The original double forge, anvils, tools, gasoline engines, belts and pulleys, and sewing machines are displayed among the various departments: blacksmith, woodworking, painting, and trimming.

In addition to the museum complex, around the town one can still locate the homes of more than two dozen buggy-shop owners and more than half a dozen buggy shops. Each has been changed and updated in this way or that over the years, but thoughtful inspection will usually reveal their earlier lives.

Although it's the history of horse-drawn buggies that draws the visitor to Mifflinburg in Union County, modern-day buggies are still a regular sight on the town's streets. The rolling countryside around the town is home to sizable Amish and Old Order Mennonite communities. In the broad valley, hundreds of them have found their answer to the pressures of suburban development that drove them from southeastern Pennsylvania. And the demand for buggies, buggy parts, and buggy repairs that they've brought with them has brought at least a few new buggy shops into operation in the area.

The Mifflinburg Buggy Days event is one of Pennsylvania's top 200 events, as selected in 1994 by the Office of Travel Marketing in the state Department of Commerce. Held each year over the Memorial Day weekend, it commemorates the period some one hundred years ago when the community was first known as "Buggy Town." Horse-drawn-buggy rides, an operating blacksmith's forge, turn-of-the-century dinner fare, fiddlers, antiques, and crafts reminiscent of the nineteenth century fill the weekend.

Mifflinburg was born Youngmanstown in 1782, the creation of Elias Youngman on a site for which he had received a patent shortly after the Revolutionary War. He came to the wilderness setting with his wife Catherine, daughter Catherine, sons George and Thomas and their families, and seven other families. By 1792 he had laid out a formal town, which extended westward from what today is Third Street, and began selling lots. The income from the sales he sank into the building of a German Reformed church and a school.

That German School House, which still stands at the corner of Fifth and Green streets, saw brief use as Union County's first courthouse in 1813, when the county was carved out of Northumberland County. But, just fourteen years later, the first county seat no longer existed as an entity unto itself. In 1827, Youngmanstown was combined with Rotestown and given the new joint name of Mifflinburg, for Pennsylvania's first governor Thomas Mifflin.

Among the most outstanding buildings in Mifflinburg is the former William Young home, today serving as Mifflinburg Borough Hall at 333 Chestnut Street. Built in 1858 on designs by Lewis Palmer, a renowned architect from nearby Lewisburg, the three-story brick building features an Italianate style with twin Victorian porches. It contrasts sharply with its contemporaries throughout the community, which were erected along the older lines popular in southwestern Pennsylvania at the time, relatively plain and strongly rectangular. It is among the most ornate and striking of Pennsylvania's municipal headquarters buildings.

A collection of historic buildings that many visitors to Mifflinburg miss stands at 401 Market Street, just a block back from the main thoroughfare. The main house on the lot was built in the 1840s, partially of bricks shipped from Philadelphia on the Pennsylvania Canal. The two smaller buildings are the original, pre–Civil War lockup for the town, which was moved here from Sixth Street, and the "Little House," a blacksmith's home built in 1808.

Back on Chestnut, at the center of town is the current home of the Scarlet D Tavern at 264 Chestnut Street. With its white-railed front porch, street-side steps, and inviting bench, the three-story tavern draws the passerby into the accommodations of another era, a time when men spent summer afternoons in rocking chairs, whittling the time away. Built in 1858, it was operated first as the Deckard House and later as the Hopp Inn and Hopp Hotel. The current owner, William Heim, took over in 1979. The current name is drawn from the colonial days of the tavern, when the tavern keeper was responsible for tallying the amount of beer each customer consumed and then making anyone who drank too much wear a placard with a scarlet D painted on it.

The restaurant decor of the Scarlet D takes the diner back to the 1800s, while still offering a casual experience that begins the moment you hear your choice of seating, "Smoking, nonsmoking, or balcony." The food is first-rate, and you never know what you'll find on the menu. Scallops are a popular main course, but there's always something like beef medallions with habañero pepper jelly, or locally raised lamb with tarragon, to tempt the adventurous.

Upstairs are a dozen hotel rooms furnished in antiques from the same period.

An 1850s atmosphere also is the goal of the Carriage Corner Restaurant at the east end of town. The menu features a good selection of home-style cooking and some home-baked breads that take me back to baking days in Mom's kitchen. Also on display, in the rafters over the front porch of the restaurant, is a collection of Mifflinburg-made buggies.

One of the most interesting specialty shops in town is Mary Koons' Heirloom Investments along Chestnut. Here hang the quilts handmade by local Amish and Old Order Mennonite women in as wide a variety and large a selection as you're likely to find. The local craftswomen also have produced large selections of other hand-sewn items, ranging from coverlets and pillows to dolls and wall hangings. The shop is housed in the former Mifflinburg Telegraph and Mifflinburg Post Office building.

Another shop is Design Tiles of Mifflinburg, just a block down Chestnut in the former Young Inn, built by William Young around 1864. Hand-painted, decorative tiles of any design the buyer can dream up are the product here. Even before you enter the shop you get a sense of the craftsmanship and utility of the tiles. They are displayed as house numbers at the building's various entrances.

Until recently Mifflinburg also could boast one of the finest remaining examples of the old-fashioned five-and-ten store. It's now Mostly Collectibles, an antiques and collectibles store, but it still has the creaky wooden floors of the old variety stores, and the original outside façade shows clearly through the more recent layers of paint. That store could only have been a five-and-ten.

Mifflinburg lies in the heart of the broad Buffalo Valley, an agricultural valley filled with eye-pleasing pastoral sights. A drive along any of the back roads of the region will help to lower the blood pressure at least a few clicks.

You'll be hard-pressed to miss the many references to buffalo in place names and the like on such a drive. There's Buffalo Crossroads, Buffalo Church, Buffalo Creek, Buffalo Road, and many more. Tradition holds that large herds of eastern bison roamed this region in the early days of European settlement. Some even swear they can take the curious to see the deep ruts worn across mountain ranges by the constant passing of the beasts. Hard evidence to support the claims has yet to be produced, although I like to hold out some hope that the wonderful tales are true. At any rate, there is at least one buffalo in the valley today, a bull in the prime of life living with a few llamas and some exotic cattle on a farm just east of Mifflinburg.

Just outside the Buffalo Valley, up over a couple hills from Mifflinburg, across the beautiful Penns Creek, and down a winding country lane, lies the internationally recognized Walnut Acres, a pioneer in organic farming. What started as a family farm in 1946 has grown into a huge mail-order operation, providing unchemicalized foods to thousands upon thousands of eager buyers.

Paul and Betty Keene moved to Walnut Acres in 1946, determined to run their farm without the chemical pesticides and fertilizers that were growing fast in popularity on farms in the post–World War II era. Rather than use chemicals, they instituted programs of building up the soil with manure and compost, keeping it strong with crop rotation, and controlling pests with strictly natural methods.

At first, harvests were meager. But the Keenes had embarked on a long-term plan for the farm and slowly it began to pay off. Yields were on the rise when a praise-filled review of the family's Apple Essence—made from unsprayed apples—appeared in a New York City newspaper. Requests from throughout the northeastern United States began to flow in. The mail-order business had begun, to the ready acceptance of the many people across the country who were searching for a source of clean foods.

Today, the operation has grown many times over. The second and third generations of the family live on the farm and work in the business. Some outside suppliers have been contracted to supplement what the farm itself can produce. But the commitment to unchemicalized food raised through earth-building and -sustaining practices has never changed.

In addition to the mail-order business, Walnut Acres now runs a well-stocked, on-site farm store that will rival any grocery store in its variety and selection. Tours of the plant are offered on weekdays, and four self-guided walking tours of the farm have been developed to show visitors what organic farming is all about.

Walnut Acres also holds various events throughout the year, including the Open House & Country Fair in August. Organic foods, wild foods, wildflowers, music, games, craft demonstrations, and all the other things that go into making a country fair are held on the farm grounds.

In 1960 Walnut Acres also created the Walnut Acres Foundation, Inc., a small, nonprofit foundation aimed at providing a simple and trustworthy outlet for the charitable impulses of the farm's customers. Every order form in every catalog carries a box for buyers to include a donation amount. All labor, office space, supplies, and the like for the operation of the foundation are provided free by Walnut Acres, allowing every cent that is donated to go to charities. Among the projects supported through the foundation are the Walnut Acres Community Center, including a preschool program; the Family Village Farm project for the homeless in India; World Hunger; and Refugee Aid.

10

Bennetts Valley: Elk Country

Even taken as a whole, the towns of Bennetts Valley add up to one of the smallest towns I've included in this book. This is the true backcountry of Pennsylvania, comprising more hunting camps and vacation homes than residences. In addition to the normal items found on convenience-store shelves everywhere, the few such stores in this region also carry items like salt blocks and mineral blocks to be used by camp owners to attract deer and elk. The human population is thin, and businesses are few and far between.

However, the drive along Route 555 from Weedville to Driftwood takes the traveler through some of the wildest and most beautiful woodlands in the state. And, at any point along this route, there's always the chance of spotting a few members of Pennsylvania's only elk herd. The only free-roaming herd east of the Mississippi River is regularly within a bull's bugle of any of these tiny towns. And with them comes a steady flow of tourists hoping to spot some of the majestic beasts. Thousands of people drive through the region each fall-bugling time. Many drive hundreds of miles to participate in the spectacle.

Under the watchful eyes of the Pennsylvania Game Commission and the Bureau of Forestry, the elk herd has grown steadily since 1988. During 1994's version of the annual aerial survey, wildlife biologists counted 224 animals. Surveys are conducted from low-flying aircraft when snow covers the ground, increasing visibility. They are usually accomplished during January and February.

The 1994 count showed an increase of 19 over the previous year's count. It was also the most wild elk in Pennsylvania at any time during the entire twentieth century. As recently as 1974, the entire herd was just 38 animals. Among the animals counted in 1994, 42 were bulls with branches to their antlers and another 11 were spike-antlered bulls. Cows numbered 117, and calves, which cannot be sexed in this type of survey, accounted for 54 of the total.

The herd also experiences some losses,. usually about 13 animals per year, and 1993–94 was no exception. The heavy blizzard of March 1993 claimed four calves. Poachers took three elk, and two succumbed to accidental injuries, including a big bull that was injured in a mating battle with another bull and died from infection. Cars claimed two animals, and a train killed one in the Mix Run area, less than a mile to the east of the area we're covering in this chapter. One elk was killed for crop damage in a local farmer's fields.

As their numbers grow, the big animals expand their

range. It currently covers about 225 square miles in Cameron and Elk counties, with Dents Run, Benezette, Medix Run, Caledonia, and Weedville forming a good bit of the southern edge. The agencies with responsibility for the elk are trying to lure the expansion into the area south and east of St. Marys, which lies to the north of our towns.

They also are trying to keep the big animals on public lands as much as possible, which helps to keep conflicts with farmers and other landowners to a minimum. Several habitat-improvement projects have been undertaken on state game lands and in state forests over the years to this end. In severe cases of crop damage, the Game Commission provides elk-deterrent fencing to the farmers.

Even as this book was going to press, the Game Commission was putting the finishing touches to a new management plan for dealing with the problems that an expanded elk herd and an expanded elk range will entail. Several options will be considered to combat problems as they arise, including—it was rumored—some limited sport hunting of a set number of the animals.

The current Pennsylvania elk herd is actually the result of a transplant effort by the Game Commission in the early part of the twentieth century. The state's native elk were extirpated in the mid-1800s. The last native elk is believed to have been shot near St. Marys in 1867. But in an effort to bring back at least a reminder of the magnificent animals, 177 Rocky Mountain elk were brought into the state and stocked into several areas that biologists felt would provide suitable habitat. Most came from Yellowstone National Park.

At first the transplanted elk flourished to the point that the Game Commission held elk-hunting seasons from 1923 to 1931, and a total of 98 antlered bulls were legally

You may catch a glimpse of an elk

taken. However, the herd then began to decline, and the season was closed as of 1932. Only the 24 released in Cameron County and 10 freed in Elk County took hold. Those animals were the ancestors of today's herd.

There's no mistaking an elk for a deer, although from time to time overexcited hunters have used this excuse when mistakenly killing elk, which are completely protected in Pennsylvania. A mature bull stands about five feet tall and weighs from 700 to 1,000 pounds. He sports a set of backward-curving antlers that can have as many as fourteen points. The cow is smaller, weighing about 500 to 600 pounds. The animal's coat varies with the season from dark brown to reddish, but it always displays a large, buff-colored patch on the rump.

Dirt roads leading north out of Benezette, onto the famed Winslow Hill, and north out of Grant are essential routes for anyone wanting a better chance at viewing elk. These roads are rough and bumpy but passable spring through fall for a car driven at slow speeds. Explore the region as a team, with one person driving and the other scanning carefully for elk, and then switching off. As big as they are, the elk do tend to blend into their environment. Trying to spot them and drive at the same time can be both fruitless and dangerous. You'll also want to make sure you carry a map that clearly shows these backroads, such as "The Elk State Forest Public Use Map" available free from the state Bureau of Forestry. Although the big animals can be seen throughout the year, September is the bugling period, when bulls gather their harems for mating. At this time of the year, the mature bulls, which spend most of their time near St. Marys, move the nine miles or so to the Winslow Hill area to join the cows.

Really ambitious elk fanciers may want to hike away from the roads to secluded clear-cut or grassy areas in May or June in hopes of spotting some of the year's new-born calf crop. The visitor's best bet for locating the elk is simply to stop in one of the local businesses and ask for directions to the most recent sightings.

Benezette or Benezett is the heart of the Pennsylvania elk country. Incidentally, you can take your pick of either spelling, just as the locals do. The Benezett Store goes sans *e*, while the adjacent and connected Benezette Restaurant employs the silent vowel. The Post Office uses the *e*. I'm told the reason for the optional spellings on the town's name—"To E or not to E," as it was explained to me—lies in long-ago differences between the township and the village. Now no one seems to be completely certain as to which was correct.

If you've ever seen the intro to the *Northern Exposure* television series, where the moose wants through the streets, you already have a fair image of the scenes with elk that regularly occur in Benezette (or Benezett). "You just pull the car over and let them pass" was the advice I was given.

Santa Claus, another figure closely associated with another species of deer, also can be found in abundance in two homes in Benezette. Jean Tuttle and her sister-in-law Helen Tuttle are the founders and artisans behind the St. Nicholas Shoppe, which isn't so much an actual shop as portions of the two women's homes. There they carve, paint, and store the wide range of wooden Santa figurines that started as a hobby but quickly grew into a flourishing business. Jean started the venture as something to make for giving to friends and relatives. When Helen was laid up recovering from a major illness, Jean urged her to do the finishing work on her carvings as a way to occupy her time and attention.

They produced what they thought would be more than enough stock for a local craft show. That stock sold out quickly, and the pair caught a glimpse of the possibilities in the enterprise, which grew into their business. Today they offer everything from three-inch-tall treetop ornaments to intricate twenty-inch figures, with an overall price range of $3 to $50.

Although Jean and Helen don't maintain a store-type operation, they might invite you into their homes for some personalized browsing, if you give them advance notice. They can be reached at 814-787-5898 or 814-787-5892. They also have a catalog.

A few miles east of Benezette, in the even smaller village of Grant, crafts, woodworking, and art by many other local artists are on display in Donnell's Gift Shop, which started twenty-three years ago as a ceramics shop. Among the gift items like those found in most gift shops everywhere, you'll also find some beautiful and well-crafted wreaths and door hangings made from local wildflowers and birch twigs.

This area also is a regular elk-sighting spot. There's a herd of about twenty that spends most of its time nearby, regularly mixing with residents' horses in their pastures.

Near the eastern terminus of our sojourn, we begin to see small wooden signs urging us to make the turn up ahead to visit the Tom Mix Birthplace Park. As we leave Route 555, we move along a twisting, turning, sometimes rough roadway that crosses the Bennett Branch of the Sinnemahoning Creek on a single-lane steel bridge and then winds back in the direction we've just come for several miles. The condition of the road, combined with the home-made appearance of the signs, may lead to thoughts of turning back before you reach the park, but I would urge you to continue. What's waiting for you just a bit further is worth the drive.

The park is the creation and the passion of Ray and Eva Flaugh, who bought the Mix homestead in 1986, when the former logging community of Mix Run had degraded into nothing more than some old foundations amid a wood-land. But they saw much more on the site and set about recovering the former homesite, root cellar, and hand-dug well. Boy Scout Troop No. 555 from nearby Emporium joined in to erect a flagpole and stone memorial in the center of the homesite.

The Flaughs also began to add new buildings on the site: the Tom Mix Comes Home Museum; the Old Barn, which houses some of the items unearthed on the site and offers many musical performances throughout the year; the Jail, a favorite photo location among visitors; and a gift shop/snack bar. On the banks of the creek are several picnic tables and fire rings for use by guests.

Each year, in mid-July, thousands of fans gather at the park for the Tom Mix Round-up, complete with a huge wagon train, all sorts of western entertainment and events, celebrity appearances, and even visits by relatives of the cowboy star. The Flaughs have tapped into an en-thusiasm for Tom Mix, the King of the Cowboys, that seems never to have died, even though the movie and radio star himself died in October 1940 in an automobile accident in Arizona.

And they've tapped in with great enthusiasm. Tours are given personally by Ray, who obviously has spent a great deal of time studying the most minute details of the cowboy star's life. For example, he points to a photo of Mix with his mother—a very rare photo because it shows Mix in a suit rather than his normal cowboy garb—and explains that the fur coat the woman is wearing cost Mix $3,000 and was made of ermine and mink.

Mix was born on the site of the park on January 6, 1880, although Hollywood publicists later created a more western birthplace for the screen legend. His family moved to DuBois when Mix was eight years old. It was there, at the age of ten, that he saw the Buffalo Bill Wild West Show and decided to go west to become a sheriff.

For a time he fulfilled that dream, working as a deputy sheriff with Will Rogers in Dewey, Oklahoma, and as a Texas Ranger. Then in 1905 he hired on at Oklahoma's 101 Wild West Ranch, where he began playing parts in the Miller Brothers Wild West Shows. He became the first great cowboy of the silver screen and, as Ray is quick to point out, "He did all his own stunts, used real bullets, and was an expert knife thrower." He made between 350 and 400 movies, was a top box-office draw, and had the largest fan club of any star.

Mix's horse, Tony, the first show horse of the movies, was almost as famous as his rider. The horse led a pampered life, getting its own hotel room when traveling and having its mane and tail permed for movie appearances.

Mix was also a radio star, sponsored by the Ralston-Purina Company on the *Tom Mix and His Ralston Straight Shooters Show.* He promoted a creed for all his "straight shooters" in the listening audience: live a life free of drugs, alcohol, and violence. When his movie career began to slow in the late 1930s, Mix began to tour with his own Tom Mix Circus.

The museum is filled with memorabilia from a career of which the merchandisers of the day obviously took full advantage. Fiction about Mix's exploits, western-themed toys of all descriptions, novelty items like decoder badges, penny-arcade photos, coloring books, games, dolls, neckerchiefs, spurs, secret-compartment belt buckles, cereal bowls, pocket knives, and many, many similar items, all denoting this or that connection with the first of the rhinestone cowboys, have been gathered here in great profusion, along with posters and photos of Mix's movies and appearances. The museum also features some memorabilia of the region from the days of the big logging operations and the native elk herds and hunts.

A few other points of interest in Bennetts Valley are the fossils found in good numbers just across the Bennett Branch of the Sinnemahoning Creek from Benezette, the Native American artifacts unearthed a bit to the east, and the ghost town upstream from the village of Dents Run.

Lumbering was big business in this region, as man moved to exploit the virgin forests of white pine, hemlock, red pine, oak, beech, sugar maple, birch, and black cherry. The first trees taken out were the huge white pines, much sought after for use as ship masts. Many enormous white pine spars were shipped to the coast between 1865 and 1872.

Hemlock, already in use for its bark in local tanneries, was the next target tree. Then sawmills and logging camps appeared throughout the region, including on the sites of many of today's small towns. They used the waterways of the area, including the Bennett Branch of the Sinnemahoning Creek, along which Route 555 runs, to float their logs to market.

These were times long before environmental awareness and conservation of resources became widespread, and the loggers pretty much destroyed the forests. Enormous wildfires often followed in the cut-over areas, destroying whatever young trees might have been left. With very few exceptions, the region was pretty much denuded. The last float of logs went down the Driftwood Branch of the Sinnemahoning Creek in 1915. The logging camps disappeared, a few leaving behind the small towns of today.

11

Gratz:
Meet Me at
the Crossroads

Like a couple of the other towns that I selected for this book, Gratz lies in the heart of a broad agricultural valley bounded on both sides by heavily wooded mountains. I guess there's something about this type of setting that speaks to me, somehow seeming to be the ideal Pennsylvania environment for a town. Perhaps it's the fact that towns in settings like this almost always have long-standing traditions focused on some unique community event or activity. In the case of Gratz, it's the Crossroads Sale and Market and the Gratz Fair.

Friday is the only day for the Crossroads Sale and Market, a few miles west of Gratz. But that feels about right, just frequent enough to make regular visits something special to look forward to and not too often to make it commonplace.

The Crossroads is a farmers' market and country auction in the true sense of those words. "It's a farmers' market, not a flea market," stresses owner Paul Leitzel. He has worked at the Crossroads nearly all his life and takes a great deal of pride in it.

Paul's father, Richard Leitzel, started the weekly market in 1931 at the Gratz Fairgrounds, on the opposite side of the borough, and moved it to the present location in 1956. The 21,000-square-foot sale and market features seventy vendors of items ranging from fresh, locally grown produce to appliances. Some vendors, such as Harris's bakery and McShane's fish sandwiches, have operated here since the 1930s.

The market is a magical, memory-filled place for a majority of us who grew up within an hour's drive or so of the spot. Brown paper bags filled—really packed—with the candy we bought for just a quarter, brightly colored chicks at Easter, buying our first little this or that for a few cents at an auction are just some of the things I remember. (Chicks may no longer legally be dyed for Easter. Laws have been changed, following allegations of high death rates following the process. But, take it from me, the survival rate for the chicks I pestered my parents into buying was very high. We filled an entire chicken coop with the white leghorn chickens they grew into. We ate the eggs that those "doomed" little peeps produced later in their lives.)

Those memories come flooding back over me today every time I find the time to make the trip (now much longer than an hour) back to the Crossroads on a Friday evening. The mingling smells of fresh produce, baked goods straight from the oven, and simmering carnival foods of all descriptions drive the nostalgia of the "homecoming" to incredible heights. Never do I come away without renewing acquaintances, sometimes with long-lost friends. The only thing that could make the experience more complete would be the sound of a couple crates of chirping peeps.

But even for those who have never visited the Crossroads previously, it's an experience worth seeking out. Although new vendors for items like vintage baseball cards and vitamins have joined the more traditional ones I remember as "always" being there, the market and auction have held fast to their origins and traditions, to those things that have kept a couple generations coming back Friday after Friday.

Leitzel says 2,000 cars have been counted here in a single day, and more people come year after year. Some bus tours have stopped. Hours are 1:00 P.M. to 10:00 P.M., with the auction beginning around 6:00.

A similarly traditional event, the Gratz Fair is one of the region's longest-running country fairs. It has been an annual September event for more than 120 years, having been formally organized in 1873.

Judging of locally raised agricultural products and crafts for ribbons and cash premiums, which has taken a backseat at many fairs across the state in recent years, remains a central part of the festivities at Gratz. The permanent display buildings are filled to overflowing with everything from jams and jellies to super pumpkins and incredible squash. Agricultural organizations, such as 4-H, still compete with educational displays as well as the livestock they've raised. The fairgrounds also play host to the Gratz Fair Craft Show in May and the Gratz Area Antique Machinery Association Annual Show in July.

Sample some farmers' market specialties

The fair is a regional event without peer in its region. Schools let students out for a day at the fair, where artwork they did back in the classrooms has been judged, awarded, and put on display. Calendars hanging on kitchen walls in homes throughout the area are marked with the dates and times of the regular grandstand features, such as sulky races, demolition derbies, and live music.

It seems that the Gratz Fair has been there forever and will always be there. There's a permanence, a continuance, about it. However, there was once a time when its future was in jeopardy. The following passage comes from the *Bi-Centennial History: Lykens-Williams Valley*, published in 1922.

"As in the course of the life of nearly every project, there arrived a time when the continuance of the Gratz Fair was held in the balance. This happened along the year 1905; at this time it was decided that the proposition was no longer a paying project and the interested parties at that time decided to discontinue it and sell the grounds in lots. The sale was commenced and several lots disposed on, when Mr. Harry Smith of Gratz, a wide-awake businessman and thoroughly experienced showman, offered to buy the grounds on the condition that the same be leased to him for a period of two years, in order that he might determine further its practicability, at the end of which period he would then purchase. This was done and it was during the years 1906–1907 that the fair was conducted under the supervision of Mr. Smith. The two-year try-out proved so wonderful a success, contingent with the injection of good clean amusements and the creation of more instilled interest in horse racing; and at the end of the period a company was organized by Mr. Smith, and the grounds taken over. Since that date keen interest manifests itself in the Gratz Fair."

That same thorough book provides the following description of the savior of the Gratz Fair:

"Mr. Smith was born in Bethlehem, Pa., and first came to the borough of Gratz in the year 1898 as a public exhibitor. In 1899 he returned to Gratz and settled in the borough permanently opening and conducting a gymnasium and engaging in amusement productions throughout the state. He is a great enthusiast for training dogs, cats, goats, etc.—and has been very successful along this line. For the past 18 years he has conducted the leading confection, soda, lunch and billiard parlor in Gratz. He has also attached to his property a large and spacious hall, in which he still exhibits first class motion picture plays, enjoying the unique distinction of being the pioneer motion picture exhibitor in the entire valley. . . . Aside from his much business, he is the patentee of several national amusement contrivances as well as the manufacturer and has shipped "The Smith Jazz Swing" as far as Australia and Canada. He is a keenly interested citizen of the borough and well respected throughout the community. Mr. Smith has been president of the Gratz Fair Association since 1908."

Gratz was founded in 1805 by its namesake Simon Gratz. However, it was Ludwig Schoffstall, moving here from Lancaster County, who built the first house on the site. It was a two-story log building, in which Conrad Frey soon came to operate one story. Frey added a tavern to the side of the store in 1820. Another of the earliest settlers in the town was John Salladay, who built a gristmill about a quarter mile north of town. The spring wheel, which stood more than twenty feet tall, was driven by a stream.

Gratz today is almost entirely a residential community. Most of the storefronts have been converted over to housing, although the former life of many of them shows through rather clearly. One that hasn't been changed is Reed's Furniture, a surprisingly large and well-stocked furniture store that has been serving the community since 1929. Joining Reed's downtown along Market Street, the main thoroughfare, are Shade's Food Market; Peddler's Junction Antique Mall, 2,000 square feet of antiques and collectibles in a former country store; the seemingly out-of-place Fuzzy Bunny nightclub; Gratz National Bank; and the Warehouse Food Outlet, with its discounted prices on a wide assortment of merchandise. And that's about it for the business community. The small museum and library of the Gratz Historical Society is also located downtown.

To the east of the town is Hegins Valley, an array of country towns surrounded by beautiful agricultural lands surrounded by wooded mountains. It's a totally nontourist setting, just right for a pleasant drive—a place of annual springtime dandelion suppers, a place where you can still find a view without a house in it. This is also another of the state's regions into which the Amish and Old Order Mennonites have fled to escape the development pressures in their former lands.

Just before the Hegins Valley wraps around the outskirts of Gratz, there is the Blyler Fruit Farm, a roadside stand of long standing offering locally grown produce and products, such as dried schnitz, which is dried apple slices used in Pennsylvania Dutch cooking. (I like to eat schnitz as a dry snack.)

When it comes to dining out in Gratz, there's only one choice and that's Reed's Inn at the east end of town. But even if there were half a dozen fine sit-down restaurants in the town, I'm certain that Reed's would still rate at the top of the list. Pennsylvania Dutch cooking is the specialty of the house and my recommendation. For dessert, try the frozen peanut butter pie.

12

Morris:
Controversy
Rattles On

The population of Morris usu-
ally stands at just 300, but three times each year that number swells many times over as all the hunting camps,
which greatly outnumber the residences, are occupied to
capacity and the few available rooms are snatched up.
Those three times of the year are the first day of deer-
hunting season in late November, the first day of trout
season in mid-April, and the annual Morris Rattlesnake
Round-Up in mid-June. (To be fair, the same can be said of
the equally tiny town of Cross Fork, just a few miles to the
southeast. That village also has a snake hunt to join deer
and trout as the big draws.)

One would expect to find an attraction like the snake
hunt listed on the various tourist directories of local events,
but the listing there of the deer and trout seasons—

statewide events—signals the importance of these to the local economy. To say that many local businesses live and die on the attraction of the region for the sportsmen of the state, and beyond, is no overstatement.

So important are these wild resources and the dollars that sportsmen are willing to spend in pursuit of them that the decisions made concerning deer management, in particular, by the Pennsylvania Game Commission are becoming highly politicized. Local state legislators from throughout the traditional deer-hunting counties of the state can be expected to appear at the meetings of the commission to give voice to the sentiments of their constituents over the lack of deer where there once were many.

This is the heart of Pennsylvania's Big Woods Country or Black Forest or northern tier. Potter County, specifically, is known as God's Country. It's a land of heavily wooded, steep mountains, where towns like Morris just seem to spring right out of the wilderness as the traveler enters them. Of Potter County's 698,880 acres, fully 88 percent are forested.

Today the remoteness also has a certain appeal for many tired and stressed urbanites elsewhere in the state, beyond those who come here to pursue fish and game. Even in the face of modern technology, this region seems to exert slowing pressures on the pace of life.

Only during the three occasions listed above does Morris take on a different, more hectic atmosphere. It's the snake hunt, begun in the mid-1950s and continuing today as one of the very oldest organized hunts in the state, that we're most concerned with here. While nearly all of the other hunts in Pennsylvania have been organized and run by snake enthusiasts and hunting organizations from outside the community, the hunt in Morris has always been a local affair, put together and run by local people.

There was a time in the early 1980s when snake hunts, both the one in Morris and those elsewhere in the state, became as politicized as deer management questions have become today. The Pennsylvania Fish Commission was moving to bring some regulation and protection to the rattlesnakes, which many conservationists felt were overhunted to the extent that the population in the state was on a downward spiral that possibly couldn't be reversed, or even stopped.

Limits were set at two rattlesnakes per hunter per day, and soon dropped to one. Sponsoring organizations were required, for the first time, to obtain permits for their hunts.

All this flew headlong into the tradition that had come to be associated with the snake hunts, and rattlesnake hunting in particular. The hunts had long been promoted as vitally necessary to remove an overabundance of the snakes from the countryside, based on tales of reptile numbers that probably never existed and reports of the snakes crawling through people's yards, which a limited number did during the mating season.

This isn't to say that the organizers of the hunts or the snake hunters themselves were bad people, spreading falsehoods to support their activities. They appear to have genuinely believed the tales and honestly feared that there were too many snakes in the vicinity of their homes for the public good. Snakes just bring out an innate fear in many people. Even today, many an otherwise enlightened outdoorsman anywhere in the state, when encountering a snake, any snake, acts on his initial impulse and kills it as quickly as he can.

The snake-hunt tradition also had grown up as the primary means of fund-raising each year to support local community organizations. In Morris, it's the Morris Township Fire Company.

Into this type of situation the politicians were sure to enter. The Fish Commission came under strong assault, being charged with trying to put an end to all organized snake hunts in the state. The agency, which must go to the legislature whenever it needs a license increase to support its programs, backed off a bit.

That left us with the situation we have today. The hunts, about a dozen of them around the state, continue today under strict regulation to provide some protection for rattlesnakes. Advocates of a total ban on the hunts, and all rattlesnake hunting, still feel that the snake population is headed into oblivion and such unneeded pressures are a primary cause.

Regardless of the controversy—and this comes from an outdoorsman who has never killed any snake he has encountered, and there have been many—the hunt remains a uniquely interesting and exciting event. In addition to the central attraction, there are always plenty of good food and additional sights to see and experience. At Morris a one-pitch softball tournament and a flea market that have been added bring in as much interest and money as the snake hunt.

The Penn Hotel Restaurant and Tavern is the only restaurant in town, and it's worth a stop around dinnertime. In addition to many fine entrees, the restaurant serves a side dish called chantilly—whipped potatoes and parsley topped with cheddar cheese—that I highly recommend.

The walls of the Penn Hotel are decorated with

greatly enlarged reprints of photographs from the heyday of the town, when a large sawmill in Morris, the world's largest tannery in nearby Hoytville, and the surrounding lumber industry provided many more jobs than are found in the region today.

Benner's General Store, one of those all-purpose country stores where you never know what you'll find, is another must-see on the Morris itinerary. Although the long string of rattlesnake rattles that the former owner, Ralph Miller, used to show to the tourists is gone, the store still displays two rattlesnake skins, each about five feet long, with the rattles still attached.

13

Lahaska:
Town
within a Town

Lahaska is actually a small country town within a small country town. And that inner town, which brings about two million visitors per year, is Peddler's Village, the creation of Earl Hart Jamison.

Peddler's Village is forty-two acres of neatly manicured landscaping and inviting brick walkways connecting seventy specialty shops. None of the generic, every-mall chain stores are here. Instead of The Gap and Foot Locker, at Peddler's Village the visitor finds the Carousel World Gift Shop, where full-size carousel animals sell for as much as $30,000; Knobs 'N Knockers, where furniture knobs and door knockers of every design are the principal fare; and Accents & Images, where country pottery is featured. Arby's and Orange Julius aren't the restaurants of choice at Peddler's Village. The menus range instead from the fine American and continental cuisine at Jenny's Restaurant to the casual but full-meal selections at The Spotted Hog to the hot dogs and pizza at Animal Crackers.

Also absent from Peddler's Village is the generic look of mall stores. The entire setting reflects the architecture of colonial America, something carried over into the overnight accommodations. The Golden Plough Inn offers sixty rooms, nearly a third of which include gas fireplaces and whirlpool baths, for those who can't manage to hit all the shops—or even all that interest them—in just one day. The rooms are scattered among six locations throughout Peddler's Village, housed above some of the stores. Compared with regular hotels or bed and breakfasts, they are on the pricey side—$95 to $300 per night— but 25,000 guests take advantage of their proximity and luxury each year.

There are many dining choices, including the weekly Murder Mystery Dinner Theater Friday and Saturday evenings in Peddler's Pub, Dixieland Brunch served Sundays in Jenny's Restaurant, a buffet-style extravaganza known as King Henry's Feast offered Thursday nights in the Cock 'n Bull Restaurant, and the Evening in the Colonial Kitchen, with cooking demonstrations and colonial-style fare on winter Mondays in the Cock 'n Bull.

Jamison launched Peddler's Village in 1962 with fourteen shops and the Cock 'n Bull restaurant on six acres that formerly had held a chicken hatchery, barn, and chicken coops. On a trip to California, he was inspired by the lively village of Carmel, which served as his model for creating the shopping village.

The tradition of lodging and entertaining the public

extends back over the generations in the Jamison family to Henry Jamison, who opened a tavern along the Buckingham Township stagecoach line in 1752. The tavern became known as the General Greene Inn in the late 1770s, named for Nathaniel Greene, who commanded the left wing of General Washington's army during the Battle of Trenton. The inn was the site at which sixteen Durham boats and flats were ordered down to McConkey's Ferry for Washington's famous crossing of the Delaware River on Christmas Day, 1776. The Golden Plough Inn at Peddler's Village today stands about a mile from the site of that former inn.

For many years the complex seemed to have peaked at forty-five shops and restaurants. But a new surge in expansion, including thirteen additions since 1989, has carried the site to its current complement of seventy specialty shops and six restaurants.

The latest addition to the complex is a restored and operating antique carousel. Housed in a glass-enclosed, air-conditioned building, each of the carousel's fifty-five wooden animals carries a value of $10,000 to $50,000. The ride was built in nearby Philadelphia in 1926, incorporating three carving styles—Coney Island, Country Fair, and Philadelphia—in the work of eight master carvers. Operated until 1985 in West Chester's Lenape Park, today it is one of only sixty such antique grand carousels remaining in the United States. Adjoining the ride is the Carousel World Museum, with a collection of carved animals, miniature carousels and amusement park rides, and other memorabilia of the great carousels of the past.

The annual Scarecrow Weekend at Peddler's Village is one of Pennsylvania's top 200 events, as selected in 1994 by the Office of Travel Marketing in the state

Stop in at the Carousel Museum

Department of Commerce. Held in September, the weekend is a country-style celebration of autumn, complete with scarecrow-making and pumpkin-painting workshops, scarecrow competition, jack-o'-lantern and gourd art contests, and festive fall foods and entertainment.

Peddler's Village also stages the Strawberry Festival in May, Art Faire in June, Teddy Bear's Picnic in July, Country Sidewalk Sale in August, Apple Festival in November (with apple butter freshly cooked over an open fire), old-time medicine shows and pie-eating contests, and Gingerbread House Competition and Display throughout the Christmas season.

Although Lahaska has been pretty much gobbled up by Peddler's Village, there are some interesting establishments that are not part of that complex. For example, the cooking enthusiast in the family will find everything from gourmet cookware to specialty cooking classes at Jacqualin Et Cie, and Native American art, particularly of our eastern woodland cultures, is offered at Ancestors. Both are along Route 202. There are also overnight accommodations off the grounds of Peddler's Village. Among these is the old Lahaska Hotel, circa 1885, which Susan and Ralph Kerney have restored and refurbished as a country inn.

Lahaska has two large complexes for antique hunters—Penn's Market & Flea Market, which houses more than fifty shops, and the Lahaska Antique Courte, with more than a dozen—and several smaller, separate shops.

The town was officially founded in 1725, but English Quakers had moved into the area of the town more than twenty years earlier, setting up the township of Buckingham on land patented to them by William Penn. In 1705 the Buckingham Meetinghouse was organized at what today is the intersection of Routes 202 and 263. The physical building was erected in 1708 by Stephen Wilson. Meeting-houses are the Quaker equivalent of both the congregation and the church in many other religions.

Wilson's construction did not meet with the approval of many members, and it was replaced in 1729. That version burned in 1767 and was replaced by the two-story stone structure that stands on the site today. Some of the benches and other furnishings inside are the originals, having been in place when the building was used as a hospital during the Revolutionary War, and the white cedar interior has never seen a coat of paint. On the grounds of the Buckingham Meetinghouse is The Strangers Plot, a cemetery that holds many Revolutionary War soldiers who died in the temporary hospital.

14

Schnecksville: A Full Social Calendar

[Author's note—Even if there weren't already plenty of reasons to include Schnecksville is this book, I would have had to invent one. After all, how many chances does a writer get to write about a town named for his family, however distant that relationship may be? Fortunately, the town has come up with lots of good reasons to deserve coverage.]

The announcement board of Community Fire Company No. 1 at the southern end of Schnecksville along Route 309 is very rarely without some listing of this or that community event. Among the biggest of these each year is Schnecksville Community Fair late in June, a full week of traditional, old-time fair, featuring baking contests and baked goods auctions, 4-H animal judging, and fireworks.

Foods available range from the traditional fair fare to the Pennsylvania Dutch cuisine of the area, including pork with sauerkraut and ham with string beans.

But if it's not the fair, it's some other event. The community and the fire company have a very active social calendar, and Fire Station No. 22 and the grounds around it very clearly show the results of all those fund-raisers. The station is a modern, four-bay affair, packed with the latest fire-fighting equipment. The complex around it includes a large kitchen and banquet hall, several additional buildings, and sports fields for the town's kids.

The fire company certainly has come a long way since it was organized on January 17, 1924, in the town's Sunday School chapel. But even way back then, the citizenry came out in force to support the organization, donating $5,280 to buy the first truck and necessary equipment. The village's school bell was put into service as the fire siren.

Before it had modern facilities, the fire company was housed in the downtown of Schnecksville, in a large stone-and-brick building that today is the Tom Hall Auction Gallery. The stone masthead on the front of the building is carved with the name of the fire company, but the interior now rings with the sound of auctioneers involved in drawing bids for auctions and estate sales throughout the year.

One hill closer to the heart of Schnecksville from the fire company's grounds is Education Park, one of the most futuristic-looking college campuses in Pennsylvania. The campus is made up of a series of low concrete-and-brick buildings, with lots of tinted windows, skylights, glass domes, and the like, spaced along wide concrete walkways lined with tightly manicured grassy areas. Bulbous street lamps appear to have come right out of some sci-fi

117

movie. The Lehigh County Community College, Lehigh County Area Vo-Tech School, and Carbon-Lehigh Intermediate Unit are all housed on various portions of the campus.

A few hills to the west lies the Trexler–Lehigh County Game Preserve, 1,100 acres of zoo, petting farm, and mini-wildlands tour. While the twenty-five-acre zoo and petting-farm portions of the preserve are similar to myriad other small zoos and menageries across the country, the tour portion sets Trexler apart. On the hillside fields and woodlands around the developed zoo area, herds of "free-roaming" bison and elk graze their way right alongside the roadway. The tour ends with a splash through a small stream running over the roadway.

Gen. Harry C. Trexler, a major benefactor to Lehigh County, established the preserve in 1906 as a personal effort to save some animal species from extinction. Committing a sizable portion of his substantial land holdings, he had bison, elk, and white-tailed deer stocked on the grounds. Originally known as Trexler Deer Park, one of the first projects on the site was the construction of thirteen miles of eight-foot-tall fencing. A few years after its creation, the park held more than 300 deer, twenty elk, and a dozen bison. Real development at the preserve began in the late 1930s with projects of the Civilian Conservation Corps, including roads, fences, and landscaping.

Nearly 100,000 people visit the preserve each year. The birthing season is a favorite time for many to stop by, in hopes of seeing a new zebra or buffalo greet the world.

Included in the park, but not pointed out to the visitors, is a relic of the long-ago days when Native Americans roamed the land around Schnecksville. The Indian Bake Oven is an oven-shaped excavation that's obviously been carved by sharp hand implements into a wall of slate rock standing about 500 feet above the Jordan Creek. It includes an oven area five feet in diameter and nine inches high, an opening for loading the material to be baked, and a top opening to allow smoke to escape. Several locals have experimented with the earthen oven over the years and found it quite capable of baking bread.

Trexler was a classic philanthropist. All through Lehigh County his donations can be seen. In addition to his substantial land donations, Trexler directed in his will that three-quarters of the income of his estate would be paid yearly to municipalities and charitable organizations in Lehigh County. He began his business career, after attending the Tremont Seminary in Norristown, New Jersey, in the lumber industry with his father and brothers. But it was not until he became involved with the Lehigh Portland Cement Co. that he acquired the large holdings in public utilities that made his fortune.

Although it's now being gobbled up by explosive residential housing development, much of the area around Schnecksville was covered at one time by large orchards. The produce of the trees was exported internationally. Among the largest orchards were those of Gen. Harry Trexler. He started them in 1906 on just five acres, but by 1933 he had 1,500 acres in production: 1,000 in apples, 300 in peaches, and the rest in pears, plums, apricots, and grapes.

Trexler never lived in Schnecksville, but his agricultural ventures sure did cover the countryside. In addition to the orchards, he had several enormous poultry plants in the area and a sheep ranch with more than 5,000 animals.

Adam Schneck held title to land at Schnecksville as early

4-H entrants at the community fair

as 1766. He came from Wurtemberg, Germany, and is said to have been the founder of the family in the region. However, it was Daniel Schneck, who laid out the town on land he owned around 1840, for whom the town is named. He and his son Moses built the first hotel as well as several other buildings. George Rau opened the first store, but eventually he sold it to Daniel Schneck, who thereafter leased it to various operators before selling it in 1843 to Joel and Peter Gross, who operated it until 1874.

Daniel ran a brick-making yard and kiln just west of the village from 1850 to 1870. Materials taken from the earth locally were used in the production. Some of the buildings in town made with Schneck's bricks are still standing.

Like most small towns of the region, Schnecksville had its carriage shop. John Hess operated the shop here from 1850 to 1862 in a large two-story brick building. Peter Salem converted the building into the Eagle Hotel in 1869.

Schnecksville was settled largely by German immigrants, who continued to use their native tongue in many of their day-to-day affairs. However, they wanted their children also to be able to use the dominant language of their new country. To that end they established the Schnecksville Academy in 1856, with the express purpose of providing a "superior English education." It was the first such school in the township. It also was the first, and for quite a while the only, school in the region to make it compulsory for only English to be spoken both in the school and on the playground. Parents paid a tuition of two and a half cents per day for their children to attend the academy.

The countryside around Schnecksville is the richest in the region with covered bridges. Five of the nostalgic old structures still carry roadways over streams within a couple of miles of the town.

And just southwest of Schnecksville lie the grounds of the Allentown–Lehigh Valley KOA Campground. During most of the year, this is a normal camping area, but around Christmas it takes on a wonderful atmosphere. Thousands of sparkling lights fill the trees, signs, and fences, and line the buildings. Dozens of life-size displays depict symbols and characters of the season. Visitors take this all in from the comfort of their vehicles as they drive around the paved loop that serves as the main roadway for campers the rest of the year. A Christmas-decoration and craft shop, with Santa for the kids, waits at the end of the drive.

Among the restaurants in Schnecksville are Yester-years Inn, with dining on an outdoor patio and some tasty seafood, and PaPa's, which features steaks, seafood, and homemade pies. Both offer good eating.

A longtime annual event in Schnecksville is the Schneck Family Reunion in August. The seventy-fifth such event was held in 1994. Organized by the Schneck Association, based of course in Schnecksville, the event attracts kith and kin from across the country for two days each year. As the association describes it, "Many out-of-town Schnecks will be coming in for the weekend to visit with us 'local Schnecks.'" A special feature is a car-caravan tour of our namesake town, which in 1994 included the earliest Schneck house, a log cabin that has been moved to the town and is being restored.

15

Shartlesville: America in Miniature

For decades Shartlesville has been known nationally as a center of Pennsylvania Dutch cooking. The reputation of local cooks, particularly those preparing the foods for local restaurants and taverns, was widespread throughout the region for generations. Then came the days of tourist travel and easy population movements across the country, and the regional reputation was carried nationwide.

The local reputation was begun by the Shartle Inn, a log tavern and restaurant that dates from the very first days that anyone referred to the town by the name of Shartlesville in 1765. More recently, a pair of restaurants have been the principal progenitors of that well-deserved reputation for the very best in chicken pot pie, ham and beans, lettuce with hot bacon dressing, stuffed pig stomach, and on and on. They are Haag's Hotel, where the cooking has been handled by the same family since the 1800s, and the Shartlesville Hotel, which has featured cooking "in the Pennsylvania Dutch tradition" since 1847.

More recently they've been joined by the Blue Mountain Family Restaurant, with specialties that include a wide range of homemade pies and cakes, by the slice on the premises or in a box to go, and the K&M Burger Ranch, which serves several wonderful variations on the burger and stands next to a statue of a giant cow holding a burger.

Equal to the fine food turned out by the restaurants in drawing national attention to this small country town is Roadside America, a tradition to travelers and residents with children for a generation. Depicting life in the rural United States from the pioneer days to the present, it's the largest indoor miniature village open to the public. And it's the creation of one man, Laurence Gieringer, a resident of the region with a lifelong passion for toy houses. His enthusiasm for things small began early in life and led to a harrowing night lost in the woods at the tender age of five.

From his bedroom window, the young Gieringer at night could see the lights of the Hilland Hotel at the crest of nearby Neversink Mountain. From his distant vantage point, those lights and that building looked like a toy he could snatch from the mountain and add to his collection of playthings. That was exactly what he set out to do one afternoon, leaving his backyard for a trek through the woods in the direction of the lights. He soon was hopelessly lost, which he remained until searchers located him the following morning.

Fortunately for all of us, Gieringer didn't let the

experience dampen his love for miniatures. As a grown-up carpenter and painter, he continued his hobby of whittling model houses, bridges, churches, and the like. Gieringer had no formal education in architectural drawing, but he arbitrarily established and religiously followed a scale of three-eighths inch to one foot in all his work.

Over sixty years Gieringer amassed quite a collection of tiny, detailed buildings and accessories, some of which he would put on display for his children and the children of neighbors and friends each Christmas. Visitors grew in number each year as word of the wondrous display spread. Then in 1935 the county's daily newspaper broke the story of Gieringer's creation to the world in a lengthy feature story. Roadside America had gone public. In 1939 through 1941, the miniature village was displayed at Carsonia Park near Reading, before being moved to its present location.

Since that time, millions of visitors have come to see the miniature zoo with its bubbling fountain, the old gristmill slowly grinding grain for flour, the trolley bumping up the side of the wooded mountain, and the half-dozen trains zipping across the landscape, over bridges, and through tunnels. Gieringer's incredible eye for detail can be seen in the replicas of real-life buildings and scenes he captured, such as the coal breaker from Locust Summit, Pennsylvania, the Pennsylvania Dutch farm from the Berks County countryside, and the Degler Chevrolet dealership from nearby Hamburg.

The 6,000-square-foot display at Roadside America was built from 21,500 feet of electrical wiring, 17,700 board feet of lumber, 6,000 feet of building paper, 4,000 feet of expanded metal under the plaster work, 2,250 feet of model railroad track, 648 feet of canvas for waterproofing,

Painting a hex sign

450 feet of pipe, 44,000 pounds of stone, 18,000 pounds of plaster, 8,000 pounds of sand, 4,000 pounds of sheet iron, 900 pounds of nails, 600 pounds of rubber roofing material for the waterways, 75 pounds of dry paint, 75 gallons of liquid paint, 225 bushels of natural moss, 25 bags of cement, three barrels of screened sawdust, and three barrels of tar. It incorporates 10,000 miniature handmade trees, 4,000 miniature figures, 600 miniature lightbulbs, 300 miniature buildings, 200 model railroad cars and engines, 96 control switches, 12 record players and amplifiers, 22 magnetic speakers, and 8 motors to make things move.

Next to Roadside America stands Dutch Haus Gifts & Snack Bar, a beautifully painted building depicting hex-sign scenes of the Pennsylvania Dutch on the outside and a selection of related souvenir, gift, and home-decor items on the inside. Hex signs, with various meanings, are available at the shop, appropriate to its location along The Hex Highway.

That's the name given to Old Route 22 from Bethel to Allentown, a thirty-four-mile stretch of highway that passes many barns and other buildings bearing the painted symbols of the Dutch country. No less than 15 structures directly along Old Route 22 carry hex signs, while more than forty others can be found along secondary roadways nearby. The route passes right through the center of Shartlesville.

Also along the hex-sign route and in Shartlesville is the Fort Motel, a lodging complex with a rustic, pioneering motif, surrounded by a replica of the walls of a pioneer fort. The motel and the Blue Mountain Family Restaurant across the street are decorated in thousands of white

Quilters at work

lights along their buildings and fences, which creates an extraordinary scene at night.

But long before any of this came to be, there was a handful of settlers on the frontier. Tradition dates the town to 1765 and Col. Peter Shartle, an officer in the Berks County Militia during the Revolutionary War. There is general agreement on the year, but there seems to be no record of Peter Shartle.

Nevertheless, there were plenty of Shartles living in the area of the town at the time that it came to be considered a town. They were the descendants of Bernard Shartle, who was born in Switzerland in 1709 and emigrated to Philadelphia in 1732. He eventually settled on 180 acres to the east of present-day Shartlesville and appeared on the county's tax rolls as early as 1754 and on the militia's "Petition for Soldiers" in 1758.

He and his wife Ursula are buried in the cemetery of St. Michael's Church, about three miles east of town. This was the first church in the area, organized as a congregation in the 1750s. In 1769, the congregation erected a log building on what today is one corner of the cemetery. The current church is the third incarnation of St. Michael's, replacing a second church in 1874.

The downtown of Shartlesville today is made up mostly of those historic and renowned restaurants already discussed, several antique shops, and an array of homes in various architectural styles, some quite old. Around the community is farming country, with various roadside produce markets selling their locally grown and made wares. The Shartlesville area has also become the focus of campers, with four campgrounds in the immediate vicinity of the town, the oldest being the Pennsylvania Dutch Campsite created in 1963.

Annual events in the town include the Shartlesville Fire Company's Annual Quilt Show & Sale in May, Painted Ladies Watermelon Festival in August, and Painted Ladies Candlelight Christmas Festival in December. Nearby Mountain Springs Camping Resort hosts an Authentic Indian Pow-Pow in August, as well as professional rodeos, demolition derbies, and monster truck shows throughout the summer.

Index

Other titles in the Country Towns series:

County Towns of Arkansas
Country Towns of Georgia
Country Towns of Michigan
Country Towns of New York
Country Towns of Northern California
Country Towns of Pennsylvania

Spring 1995
Country Towns of Connecticut and Rhode Island
Country Towns of Florida
Country Towns of Louisiana
Country Towns of Maine
Country Towns of Southern California
Country Towns of Texas

All books are $9.95 at bookstores.
Or order directly from the publisher (add $3.00 shipping and
handling for direct orders):

Country Roads Press
P.O. Box 286
Castine, Maine 04421
Toll-free phone number: **800-729-9179**